Better Practice Better Golf

Short Game Practice Workbook

Better Practice Better Golf

Short Game Practice Workbook

Dr. Nicky Lumb PhD
PGA Professional

Better Practice Better Golf Short Game Workbook is a practical, step-by-step guide to optimising your practice on all shots off the green inside 125 yards. Its flexible design will suit every player from recreational golfer to elite amateur and tour pro. It is one of six workbooks that compliments the book Better Practice Better Golf by Dr Nicky Lumb and Dr Dave Alred MBE.

Books in the Better Practice Better Golf series:
Better Practice Better Golf
Putting Workbook
Short Game Workbook
Long Game Workbook
On the Course Workbook
Pre and Post Shot Routine Workbook
Performance and Playing Statistics Workbook

Better Practice Better Golf

betterpracticebettergolf.com

First published in Great Britain in 2021 by Blue Horizon Publishing, a division of Blue Horizon Digital Solutions Ltd - bluehorizondigital.co.uk

ISBN 978-1-914321-13-9

A CIP catalogue record for this book is available from the British Library.

10 9 8 7 6 5 4 3 2 1

CONTENTS

INTRODUCTION

Better Practice Better Golf Short Game Workbook focuses on all shots off the green inside 125-yards. It is divided into two sections; shots inside 50 yards and shots between 50 and 125 yards. Inside 30-yards, practices are in 10-yard bands e.g., 10-20 and 20-30 yards. For distances over 50-yards, yardages are in 25-yard increments e.g., 50-75 and 75-100 yards.

On the course, most approach shots that miss the green finish within 20-yards of it, so many of the practices focus on green side shots inside this range. If there is a distance band you play from more often, you can adapt any practice so it better suits your needs.

Training and Tournament Practices

There are two types of practices in this workbook: training and tournament.

Training practice helps to develop your ball control so that you learn to get more shots closer to the hole. It involves playing games with scoring systems and recording and monitoring your scores so that you see your skills improve over time.

Tournament practice more closely replicates playing golf and is 'one shot one opportunity.' It involves adding a consequence to your practice and scoring every shot so that you practice performing under pressure. This is the ultimate test in determining whether the skills you learned or refined during your practice are likely to hold up in competition. Usually, the more often a shot matches your intention, the better your skills will transfer onto the golf course and into competition.

Shot Difficulty

On the course, short game shots vary in difficulty. Some shots will be straight forward from good fairway lies with plenty of green to work with. Other shots will be from poor lies with carries over water or sand with little green to work with. Every practice starts with good lies in the fairway or sand, so you can focus on achieving a good strike. As you progress, vary your lies so that you practice from the rough and awkward lies as well. Your practice should represent the full variety of shots you will face on the course.

Shot Making / Playing Different Shots

With short game shots, we often have to be creative and change the trajectory and height so that some shots fly higher and others lower. Sometimes you will need the ball to stop quickly; on other occasions, you will want more roll. You can do this by using clubs with more loft for higher shots and less loft for lower ones.

Moving the ball forwards in your stance will shallow your attack angle, increase the amount of loft delivered to the ball and engage more bounce (angle between the leading edge and trailing edge of the club head), making the ball fly higher. Moving the ball position backwards has the opposite effect. It steepens the angle of attack, reduces the amount of loft delivered, engages more of the leading edge and uses less bounce so that the ball flies lower and runs more. Opening the club face also influences the ball's flight, roll and spin. Some shots will need just one of these interventions, while others will require more.

Surf the Turf

For standard short game shots, a good strike is usually achieved when the club face strikes the ball just before it lightly brushes the ground. This makes impact a slight downward strike, with the lowest point of the swing just after the club face has hit the ball. It's important that the club head doesn't dig into the ground, so try to feel the club 'surf the turf.' Using the bounce can help you as it increases forgiveness so you get better results from less than perfect strikes.

Using Different Clubs

Many golfers play most of their shots around the green with one or two wedges so they can build strong feels. If you often use more than one club to play a shot, change clubs at any time and mark this on the scorecard. By recording your scores, you will know which wedge is most accurate. It is also beneficial to practice with other clubs at times so that you become more adaptable and can call upon an array of shot options.

Scorecards

Each practice has a score card to fill in to encourage you to be accountable for every shot, just as you are on the course. The scorecards will help you to monitor your performances and progress over time.

Towards the back of the workbook there are a number of On the Course practices. You can enter your scores directly into this workbook while you are playing, or write them on a scorecard so it's less cumbersome, before transferring your data into the workbook after your round.

Personal Bests

Every practice is scorable and has a space for Personal Bests so you can keep them up to date. This will give you a target score to aim to beat every time you practice, and will help to make your practice more productive and fun.

At the back of the workbook there is a Personal Best section for you to enter your first personal best and final score. Hopefully you will make great progress!

Celebrate Success

Every time you set a new personal best, be proud of your progress and celebrate your success! The more success you have, the more successful you will see yourself as being. This will have a cumulative effect on building momentum and helping you to get better.

Challenge

You will probably find some of the practices much harder than others, and a few very difficult. If any practice is currently too challenging, you can adapt it by reducing the target score. Always remember that you get the most benefit when you mentally apply yourself to a shot and when you do this, your brain still learns, even if you don't succeed. Signs of improvement usually take time and often much longer than we would like, so do your best to give every shot your full attention.

For your practice to be most effective, it must challenge you. Many of the practices have different levels so if a practice feels easy, or if you are regularly achieving new personal bests and feel ready for a harder, more demanding practice, move to the next level.

The challenge of any practice can be increased by working on two shot types at the same time, and alternating between shots or sets of shots, e.g. chipping and putting. On the course, you rarely use the same club for consecutive shots unless you are putting, so by doing this in practice, you will become more adaptable and better prepared to play golf.

Most golfers stop improving because they don't push themselves when they practice, so aim to give the same amount of effort to achieving scores in practice that you give when you are competing on the course. Always make your practice challenging, and remember, if it doesn't challenge you, it will not improve you as much.

Time Management

Time is valuable, so make the most of it by planning your practice sessions in advance and deciding which practices you will do.

Mix it Up

To maintain your mental engagement, mix up the practices so you do not spend too long on any one practice. If the facilities allow, do a short game practice followed by a putting practice and then a long game one, and then repeat the cycle. You can take this a step closer to replicating playing golf by working on two practices at once, and playing one short game shot or a set of shots before doing one putt or one set of putts. We tend to remember more about the beginning and end of a session than the middle part, so it's beneficial to keep practices short and sharp.

Notes

With every scorecard there is a small notes section for you to write down any thoughts or feelings that occurred during your practice. If the notes area isn't big enough, there are a number of blank pages at the end of the workbook.

Review and Reflect

It's beneficial to always review your practice. The notes section and blank pages at the end of the workbook provide space to record what went well and what you can do to be better next time.

Attitude and Application

What you do in practice will influence your progress, and so will how you do it. Two people can do exactly the same practice. One person can hit each shot with a clear intention and give every ball their full attention. Another player can go through the motions mindlessly hitting. When this happens, it's not difficult to guess who will make the most progress. If you have the same desire and determination to achieve scores in practice that you have when you are competing on the course, you will reap the rewards.

Your attitude influences everything you do, so always do your best. Be patient and persistent. The road to improvement is full of highs, lows and plateaus. It will never be a smooth ride, but a good, productive attitude and systematically following and building on the practices in this workbook will accelerate your progress and help you to play better golf.

You don't need to be able to hit the ball over 300 yards to have a good short game, so everyone can improve! Enjoy turning better practice into better golf. Today is your opportunity to start to see just how good you can be!

Short Game Statistics

The Short Game Chart on page 15 shows the main short game categories that contribute to a total score at the end of a round. The leading score in each shot category on the PGA Tour is listed first, followed by the tour average. You will see that amongst the world's best players there can be fairly big differences in their skill levels.

The purpose of practice is to improve your skills and shoot lower scores on the course. To do this, you need to know where you are now so that you always have scores to beat and can measure and monitor your progress over time.

Knowing your average proximity to the hole from each distance can help you to set realistic shot expectations, make it easier to manage your emotions, reduce your frustrations and increase your enjoyment on the course.

It's most accurate to determine your current skill levels by recording and then analysing your on-course playing statistics. If you don't have this information then the practices in Your Short Game Statistics Section will help you to do this. The Track Your Own Short Game Chart on page 16 will help you to monitor your scores over time.

Once you have worked out your scores, you will have a baseline and can set goals to improve them. You can also be realistic with your short game shot expectations on the course.

Dr Nicky Lumb

Short Game

Distance to Hole	Proximity to Hole		Your Score	Your Goal
	Best Average	PGA Tour Average		
< 10yds	2ft	4ft		
10-20yds	6ft	7ft		
20-30yds	7ft	9ft		
> 30 yds	8ft	12ft		
Sand Shots*	7ft	10ft		

Up and Downs

Distance to Hole	Highest Average	PGA Tour Average	Your Score	Your Goal
< 10yds	2ft	4ft		
10-20yds	6ft	7ft		
20-30yds	7ft	9ft		
> 30 yds	8ft	12ft		
Sand Saves*	7ft	10ft		

* from Greenside Bunkers

Approach Shots

Distance to Hole	Proximity to Hole			Your Score (Fwy)	Your Goal
	Best Average	PGA Tour Average	Rough**		
50-75yds	9ft	17ft	25ft		
75-100yds	13ft	18ft	27ft		
100-125yds	16ft	20ft	31ft		

Statistics from the PGA Tour 2019 season. **The proximity to the hole from the rough is shown to illustrate the differences in accuracy when a player hits a shot into a green from the rough instead of the fairway.

Track Your Own Short Game

Distance to Hole	Proximity to Hole					
	Date	Date	Date	Date	Date	Date
< 10yds						
10-20yds						
20-30yds						
> 30 yds						
Sand Shots						

Up and Downs	Date	Date	Date	Date	Date	Date
< 10yds						
10-20yds						
20-30yds						
> 30 yds						
Sand Saves						

Approach Shots	Proximity to Hole					
	Date	Date	Date	Date	Date	Date
50-75yds						
75-100yds						
100-125yds						

Dr Nicky Lumb

Plan and Picture Every Shot

Before you play any shot, always choose a small, precise landing spot. See in your mind exactly what you want the ball to do and where you want it to go from the moment it comes off your club face, to where and how it lands and reaches the hole.

Be attentive to where and how every ball lands in relation to your intention, so you can learn from every shot you hit.

Your Short Game Statistics

The purpose of practice is to improve your skills and shoot lower scores on the course. To do this, you need to know where you are now so that you always have scores to beat, and can measure and monitor your progress.

Proximity to the Hole and Up and Downs

- Play to a hole within 10 yards.

- Measure the distance the ball finishes from the hole and enter it onto the scorecard.

- Try to hole the putt. If you hole it, place a tick in the Up and Down (↑ & ↓) box.

- Repeat this process from different fairway positions inside 10 yards for 10 shots. Vary the type of shots so that you play a variety of chip and lob shots. Always use the club you feel will give you the best result.

- To get the most accurate representation of what your accuracy will be on the course, hit a full shot between each short game shot or measure a couple of shot categories at the same time.

- Calculate your average proximity to the hole for each distance band by dividing the total distance by 10.

- Calculate your up and down percentage by totalling your successes and multiplying your score by 10.

- Repeat from 10-20 yards, 20-30 yards, 30-50 yards and inside 20 yards from good sand lies in a bunker. This can take a number of sessions to complete properly.

- Record your scores in the Track Your Own Short Game Chart on page 16.

- Repeat this exercise regularly. Aim to increase your accuracy and improve your scores over time.

Dr Nicky Lumb

Proximity to the Hole & Up and Downs										Date:		
Dist. from Hole	1	2	3	4	5	6	7	8	9	10	Total	Avg
<10yds												
< 10yds ↑ & ↓												
10-20yds												
10-20yds ↑ & ↓												
20-30yds												
20-30yds ↑ & ↓												
30-50yds												
30-50yds ↑ & ↓												
Sand <20yds												
< 20yds ↑ & ↓												

Proximity to the Hole & Up and Downs										Date:		
Dist. from Hole	1	2	3	4	5	6	7	8	9	10	Total	Avg
<10yds												
< 10yds ↑ & ↓												
10-20yds												
10-20yds ↑ & ↓												
20-30yds												
20-30yds ↑ & ↓												
30-50yds												
30-50yds ↑ & ↓												
Sand <20yds												
< 20yds ↑ & ↓												

Proximity to the Hole & Up and Downs										Date:		
Dist. from Hole	1	2	3	4	5	6	7	8	9	10	Total	Avg
<10yds												
< 10yds ↑ & ↓												
10-20yds												
10-20yds ↑ & ↓												
20-30yds												
20-30yds ↑ & ↓												
30-50yds												
30-50yds ↑ & ↓												
Sand <20yds												
< 20yds ↑ & ↓												

Proximity to the Hole & Up and Downs										Date:		
Dist. from Hole	1	2	3	4	5	6	7	8	9	10	Total	Avg
<10yds												
< 10yds ↑ & ↓												
10-20yds												
10-20yds ↑ & ↓												
20-30yds												
20-30yds ↑ & ↓												
30-50yds												
30-50yds ↑ & ↓												
Sand <20yds												
< 20yds ↑ & ↓												

Dr Nicky Lumb

Proximity to the Hole & Up and Downs										Date:		
Dist. from Hole	1	2	3	4	5	6	7	8	9	10	Total	Avg
<10yds												
< 10yds ↑ & ↓												
10-20yds												
10-20yds ↑ & ↓												
20-30yds												
20-30yds ↑ & ↓												
30-50yds												
30-50yds ↑ & ↓												
Sand <20yds												
< 20yds ↑ & ↓												

Proximity to the Hole & Up and Downs										Date:		
Dist. from Hole	1	2	3	4	5	6	7	8	9	10	Total	Avg
<10yds												
< 10yds ↑ & ↓												
10-20yds												
10-20yds ↑ & ↓												
20-30yds												
20-30yds ↑ & ↓												
30-50yds												
30-50yds ↑ & ↓												
Sand <20yds												
< 20yds ↑ & ↓												

Distance Band Proximities to the Hole

- Select a hole or target at 75 yards.

- Place 10 balls between 50 and 75 yards so one ball is every 2 to 3 yards. E.g., 50, 53, 56 and 59 yards etc.

- To get a more accurate representation of what your accuracy will be on the course, take time between each shot to hole a four-feet putt or play a short chip shot.

- Measure the distance each ball finishes from the target and enter it onto the scorecard.

- Calculate your average proximity to the hole by dividing the total distance by 10.

- Repeat from 75-100 yards and 100-125 yards. This can take a number of sessions to complete properly.

- Record your scores in the Track Your Own Short Game Chart on page 16.

- Repeat this exercise regularly. Aim to improve your accuracy and reduce your average proximity distances over time.

Proximity to the Hole										Date:		
Dist. from Hole	1	2	3	4	5	6	7	8	9	10	Total	Avg
50-75yds												
75-100yds												
100-125yds												

Proximity to the Hole										Date:		
Dist. from Hole	*1*	*2*	*3*	*4*	*5*	*6*	*7*	*8*	*9*	*10*	*Total*	*Avg*
50-75yds												
75-100yds												
100-125yds												

Proximity to the Hole										Date:		
Dist. from Hole	*1*	*2*	*3*	*4*	*5*	*6*	*7*	*8*	*9*	*10*	*Total*	*Avg*
50-75yds												
75-100yds												
100-125yds												

Proximity to the Hole										Date:		
Dist. from Hole	*1*	*2*	*3*	*4*	*5*	*6*	*7*	*8*	*9*	*10*	*Total*	*Avg*
50-75yds												
75-100yds												
100-125yds												

Proximity to the Hole										Date:		
Dist. from Hole	*1*	*2*	*3*	*4*	*5*	*6*	*7*	*8*	*9*	*10*	*Total*	*Avg*
50-75yds												
75-100yds												
100-125yds												

Proximity to the Hole										Date:		
Dist. from Hole	*1*	*2*	*3*	*4*	*5*	*6*	*7*	*8*	*9*	*10*	*Total*	*Avg*
50-75yds												
75-100yds												
100-125yds												

CHIPPING

TRAINING PRACTICES

The following training practices will help you to develop your short game skills. To move any practice closer to a tournament practice, hit a full shot before a short game shot so your practice more closely represents what you do on the course.

Landing Spots

Being able to land a ball on an intended spot will develop your striking consistency, and knowing how it is likely to react on landing, and how much it is likely to roll is important for good chipping. With a 58 or 60-degree wedge, the ball will usually fly higher and stop quickly. With a pitching wedge, which has less loft, the ball will fly much lower and run more.

Equipment: Wedges, balls, 4 or 5 tees, coin or scorecard, workbook, pen

- Place a coin on a green 5 yards from the edge. If you struggle to see a coin, use a scorecard and secure it with a tee.
- Put tees at 12, 3, 6 and 9 o'clock 3ft around the coin. Based on your skill level, from 20 yards or more, place the tees 6ft from the coin if you need to. (For measuring purposes, a wedge is about 3ft).
- Before every shot, visualise the ball landing on the coin.
- From different fairway positions at 5 yards, how many shots does it take to land 3 balls inside the marked area?

Dr Nicky Lumb

- Complete the scorecard.

- Note how far each ball rolls once it has landed. This will help you determine where shots need to land to reach targets in the future.

- Repeat from 10, 15, 20, 30 and 40 yards.

- If you usually use more than one wedge, repeat this practice using the clubs you would often use so you can compare their accuracy.

- Record your scores and next time aim to land 3 balls in each scoring zone in one shot less. Every time you set a new personal best, write it down. Be proud of your progress and celebrate your success!

- If you start at 6ft from 20 yards, aim to gradually reduce the size of the scoring zone over time.

PB Date:							
Total Shots							
PB Date:							
Total Shots							

Landing Spots						
Date:	5yds	10yds	15yds	20yds	30yds	40yds
Target Size	3ft	3ft	3ft	3ft / 6ft	3ft / 6ft	3ft / 6 ft
Club:						
Club:						
Notes:					Total Shots	

Landing Spots

Date:	5yds	10yds	15yds	20yds	30yds	40yds
Target Size	3ft	3ft	3ft	3ft / 6ft	3ft / 6ft	3ft / 6 ft
Club:						
Club:						

Notes:

Total Shots

Date:	5yds	10yds	15yds	20yds	30yds	40yds
Target Size	3ft	3ft	3ft	3ft / 6ft	3ft / 6ft	3ft / 6 ft
Club:						
Club:						

Notes:

Total Shots

Date:	5yds	10yds	15yds	20yds	30yds	40yds
Target Size	3ft	3ft	3ft	3ft / 6ft	3ft / 6ft	3ft / 6 ft
Club:						
Club:						

Notes:

Total Shots

Date:	5yds	10yds	15yds	20yds	30yds	40yds
Target Size	3ft	3ft	3ft	3ft / 6ft	3ft / 6ft	3ft / 6 ft
Club:						
Club:						

Notes:

Total Shots

Dr Nicky Lumb

Landing Spots

Date:	5yds	10yds	15yds	20yds	30yds	40yds
Target Size	3ft	3ft	3ft	3ft / 6ft	3ft / 6ft	3ft / 6 ft
Club:						
Club:						
Notes:				Total Shots		

Date:	5yds	10yds	15yds	20yds	30yds	40yds
Target Size	3ft	3ft	3ft	3ft / 6ft	3ft / 6ft	3ft / 6 ft
Club:						
Club:						
Notes:				Total Shots		

Date:	5yds	10yds	15yds	20yds	30yds	40yds
Target Size	3ft	3ft	3ft	3ft / 6ft	3ft / 6ft	3ft / 6 ft
Club:						
Club:						
Notes:				Total Shots		

Date:	5yds	10yds	15yds	20yds	30yds	40yds
Target Size	3ft	3ft	3ft	3ft / 6ft	3ft / 6ft	3ft / 6 ft
Club:						
Club:						
Notes:				Total Shots		

Landing Spots

Date:	5yds	10yds	15yds	20yds	30yds	40yds
Target Size	3ft	3ft	3ft	3ft / 6ft	3ft / 6ft	3ft / 6 ft
Club:						
Club:						
Notes:					Total Shots	

Date:	5yds	10yds	15yds	20yds	30yds	40yds
Target Size	3ft	3ft	3ft	3ft / 6ft	3ft / 6ft	3ft / 6 ft
Club:						
Club:						
Notes:					Total Shots	

Date:	5yds	10yds	15yds	20yds	30yds	40yds
Target Size	3ft	3ft	3ft	3ft / 6ft	3ft / 6ft	3ft / 6 ft
Club:						
Club:						
Notes:					Total Shots	

Date:	5yds	10yds	15yds	20yds	30yds	40yds
Target Size	3ft	3ft	3ft	3ft / 6ft	3ft / 6ft	3ft / 6 ft
Club:						
Club:						
Notes:					Total Shots	

Dr Nicky Lumb

Landing Spots

Date:	5yds	10yds	15yds	20yds	30yds	40yds
Target Size	3ft	3ft	3ft	3ft / 6ft	3ft / 6ft	3ft / 6 ft
Club:						
Club:						

Notes:	Total Shots

Date:	5yds	10yds	15yds	20yds	30yds	40yds
Target Size	3ft	3ft	3ft	3ft / 6ft	3ft / 6ft	3ft / 6 ft
Club:						
Club:						

Notes:	Total Shots

Date:	5yds	10yds	15yds	20yds	30yds	40yds
Target Size	3ft	3ft	3ft	3ft / 6ft	3ft / 6ft	3ft / 6 ft
Club:						
Club:						

Notes:	Total Shots

Date:	5yds	10yds	15yds	20yds	30yds	40yds
Target Size	3ft	3ft	3ft	3ft / 6ft	3ft / 6ft	3ft / 6 ft
Club:						
Club:						

Notes:	Total Shots

Landing Spots

Date:	5yds	10yds	15yds	20yds	30yds	40yds
Target Size	3ft	3ft	3ft	3ft / 6ft	3ft / 6ft	3ft / 6 ft
Club:						
Club:						
Notes:				Total Shots		

Date:	5yds	10yds	15yds	20yds	30yds	40yds
Target Size	3ft	3ft	3ft	3ft / 6ft	3ft / 6ft	3ft / 6 ft
Club:						
Club:						
Notes:				Total Shots		

Date:	5yds	10yds	15yds	20yds	30yds	40yds
Target Size	3ft	3ft	3ft	3ft / 6ft	3ft / 6ft	3ft / 6 ft
Club:						
Club:						
Notes:				Total Shots		

Date:	5yds	10yds	15yds	20yds	30yds	40yds
Target Size	3ft	3ft	3ft	3ft / 6ft	3ft / 6ft	3ft / 6 ft
Club:						
Club:						
Notes:				Total Shots		

Dr Nicky Lumb

Landing Spots

Date:	5yds	10yds	15yds	20yds	30yds	40yds
Target Size	3ft	3ft	3ft	3ft / 6ft	3ft / 6ft	3ft / 6 ft
Club:						
Club:						
Notes:				Total Shots		

Date:	5yds	10yds	15yds	20yds	30yds	40yds
Target Size	3ft	3ft	3ft	3ft / 6ft	3ft / 6ft	3ft / 6 ft
Club:						
Club:						
Notes:				Total Shots		

Date:	5yds	10yds	15yds	20yds	30yds	40yds
Target Size	3ft	3ft	3ft	3ft / 6ft	3ft / 6ft	3ft / 6 ft
Club:						
Club:						
Notes:				Total Shots		

Date:	5yds	10yds	15yds	20yds	30yds	40yds
Target Size	3ft	3ft	3ft	3ft / 6ft	3ft / 6ft	3ft / 6 ft
Club:						
Club:						
Notes:				Total Shots		

Landing Spots

Date:	5yds	10yds	15yds	20yds	30yds	40yds
Target Size	3ft	3ft	3ft	3ft / 6ft	3ft / 6ft	3ft / 6 ft
Club:						
Club:						
Notes:				Total Shots		

Date:	5yds	10yds	15yds	20yds	30yds	40yds
Target Size	3ft	3ft	3ft	3ft / 6ft	3ft / 6ft	3ft / 6 ft
Club:						
Club:						
Notes:				Total Shots		

Date:	5yds	10yds	15yds	20yds	30yds	40yds
Target Size	3ft	3ft	3ft	3ft / 6ft	3ft / 6ft	3ft / 6 ft
Club:						
Club:						
Notes:				Total Shots		

Date:	5yds	10yds	15yds	20yds	30yds	40yds
Target Size	3ft	3ft	3ft	3ft / 6ft	3ft / 6ft	3ft / 6 ft
Club:						
Club:						
Notes:				Total Shots		

Dr Nicky Lumb

Landing Spots

Date:	5yds	10yds	15yds	20yds	30yds	40yds
Target Size	3ft	3ft	3ft	3ft / 6ft	3ft / 6ft	3ft / 6 ft
Club:						
Club:						

Notes:			Total Shots	

Date:	5yds	10yds	15yds	20yds	30yds	40yds
Target Size	3ft	3ft	3ft	3ft / 6ft	3ft / 6ft	3ft / 6 ft
Club:						
Club:						

Notes:			Total Shots	

Date:	5yds	10yds	15yds	20yds	30yds	40yds
Target Size	3ft	3ft	3ft	3ft / 6ft	3ft / 6ft	3ft / 6 ft
Club:						
Club:						

Notes:			Total Shots	

Date:	5yds	10yds	15yds	20yds	30yds	40yds
Target Size	3ft	3ft	3ft	3ft / 6ft	3ft / 6ft	3ft / 6 ft
Club:						
Club:						

Notes:			Total Shots	

Landing Spots – How Far Can You Go?

Equipment: Wedges, balls, 4 or 5 tees, coin or scorecard, workbook, pen

Level 1

- Place a coin on a green 5 yards from the edge (use a scorecard if a coin is too small to see).

- Put tees at 12, 3, 6 and 9 o'clock 3ft around the coin.

- Hit from fairway grass.

- When 3 balls have landed in the marked area, hole one four-foot putt, then move three yards back and repeat from 8 yards.

- Always hole one four-foot putt before moving three yards further back.

- Set a time limit, e.g. 15 minutes. How far back can you go?

Level 2

- Use Level 1's method.

- Every time 3 consecutive shots land in the marked area, attempt to hole one four-foot putt. If you hole it, move three yards further back and repeat from 8 yards. If you miss the putt, go back to the distance you just played from.

- Set a time limit, e.g. 15 minutes. How far back can you go?

- If you consistently reach a certain distance such as 14 yards and struggle to get further back, adapt the practice and start your next session at 11 yards so you are always working at the edge of your current ability.

Record your scores and next time aim to get three yards further back. Every time you set a new personal best, write it down. Be proud of your progress and celebrate your success!

Dr Nicky Lumb

PB Date:							
Level 1							

PB Date:							
Level 2							

Landing Spots - How Far Can You Go?		
Date	**Time**	**Distance**
Date:		
L1 L2 ☐ ☐	Notes:	
Date:		
L1 L2 ☐ ☐	Notes:	
Date:		
L1 L2 ☐ ☐	Notes:	
Date:		
L1 L2 ☐ ☐	Notes:	
Date:		
L1 L2 ☐ ☐	Notes:	

Landing Spots - How Far Can You Go?		
Date	**Time**	**Distance**
Date:		
L1 L2 ☐ ☐	Notes:	
Date:		
L1 L2 ☐ ☐	Notes:	
Date:		
L1 L2 ☐ ☐	Notes:	
Date:		
L1 L2 ☐ ☐	Notes:	
Date:		
L1 L2 ☐ ☐	Notes:	
Date:		
L1 L2 ☐ ☐	Notes:	
Date:		
L1 L2 ☐ ☐	Notes:	

Dr Nicky Lumb

Landing Spots - How Far Can You Go?		
Date	**Time**	**Distance**
Date:		
L1 ☐ L2 ☐	Notes:	
Date:		
L1 ☐ L2 ☐	Notes:	
Date:		
L1 ☐ L2 ☐	Notes:	
Date:		
L1 ☐ L2 ☐	Notes:	
Date:		
L1 ☐ L2 ☐	Notes:	
Date:		
L1 ☐ L2 ☐	Notes:	
Date:		
L1 ☐ L2 ☐	Notes:	

Landing Spots - How Far Can You Go?		
Date	**Time**	**Distance**
Date:		
L1 L2 ☐ ☐	Notes:	
Date:		
L1 L2 ☐ ☐	Notes:	
Date:		
L1 L2 ☐ ☐	Notes:	
Date:		
L1 L2 ☐ ☐	Notes:	
Date:		
L1 L2 ☐ ☐	Notes:	
Date:		
L1 L2 ☐ ☐	Notes:	
Date:		
L1 L2 ☐ ☐	Notes:	

Landing Spots - How Far Can You Go?		
Date	**Time**	**Distance**
Date:		
L1 L2 ☐ ☐	Notes:	
Date:		
L1 L2 ☐ ☐	Notes:	
Date:		
L1 L2 ☐ ☐	Notes:	
Date:		
L1 L2 ☐ ☐	Notes:	
Date:		
L1 L2 ☐ ☐	Notes:	
Date:		
L1 L2 ☐ ☐	Notes:	
Date:		
L1 L2 ☐ ☐	Notes:	

Chip and Runs – How Far Can You Go?

Your next shot will always be played where your ball finishes, so it's important to get the ball to finish as close to the target as possible.

Equipment: Wedges, balls, 4 tees, putter, workbook, pen

Level 1

- Choose a hole 10 yards from the edge of the green.

- Put tees at 12, 3, 6 and 9 o'clock 3ft around the hole.

- Hit from fairway grass.

- Play every ball as it lies.

- When 3 balls finish inside the marked area, hole one four-foot putt, then move three yards back and repeat from 13 yards.

- Always hole one four-foot putt before moving three yards further back.

- Set a time limit, e.g. 15 minutes. How far back can you go?

Level 2

- Use Level 1's method.

- Every time 3 consecutive shots finish inside the marked area, attempt to hole one four-foot putt. If you hole it, move three yards further back and repeat from 13 yards. If you miss the putt, go back to the distance you just chipped from.

- Set a time limit, e.g. 15 minutes. How far back can you go?

- If you consistently reach a certain distance such as 19 yards and struggle to get further back, adapt the practice and start your next session at 16 yards so you are always working at the edge of your current ability.

Record your scores and next time aim to get three yards further back. Every time you set a new personal best, write it down. Be proud of your progress and celebrate your success!

PB Date:							
Level 1							
PB Date:							
Level 2							

Chip and Runs – How Far Can You Go?		
Date	**Time**	**Distance**
Date:		
L1 L2 ☐ ☐	Notes:	
Date:		
L1 L2 ☐ ☐	Notes:	
Date:		
L1 L2 ☐ ☐	Notes:	
Date:		
L1 L2 ☐ ☐	Notes:	

Chip and Runs – How Far Can You Go?		
Date	**Time**	**Distance**
Date:		
L1 ☐ L2 ☐	Notes:	
Date:		
L1 ☐ L2 ☐	Notes:	
Date:		
L1 ☐ L2 ☐	Notes:	
Date:		
L1 ☐ L2 ☐	Notes:	
Date:		
L1 ☐ L2 ☐	Notes:	
Date:		
L1 ☐ L2 ☐	Notes:	
Date:		
L1 ☐ L2 ☐	Notes:	

Chip and Runs – How Far Can You Go?		
Date	**Time**	**Distance**
Date:		
L1 L2 ☐ ☐	Notes:	
Date:		
L1 L2 ☐ ☐	Notes:	
Date:		
L1 L2 ☐ ☐	Notes:	
Date:		
L1 L2 ☐ ☐	Notes:	
Date:		
L1 L2 ☐ ☐	Notes:	
Date:		
L1 L2 ☐ ☐	Notes:	
Date:		
L1 L2 ☐ ☐	Notes:	

Chip and Runs – How Far Can You Go?		
Date	**Time**	**Distance**
Date:		
L1 L2 ☐ ☐	Notes:	
Date:		
L1 L2 ☐ ☐	Notes:	
Date:		
L1 L2 ☐ ☐	Notes:	
Date:		
L1 L2 ☐ ☐	Notes:	
Date:		
L1 L2 ☐ ☐	Notes:	
Date:		
L1 L2 ☐ ☐	Notes:	
Date:		
L1 L2 ☐ ☐	Notes:	

Chip and Runs – How Far Can You Go?		
Date	**Time**	**Distance**
Date:		
L1 L2 ☐ ☐	Notes:	
Date:		
L1 L2 ☐ ☐	Notes:	
Date:		
L1 L2 ☐ ☐	Notes:	
Date:		
L1 L2 ☐ ☐	Notes:	
Date:		
L1 L2 ☐ ☐	Notes:	
Date:		
L1 L2 ☐ ☐	Notes:	
Date:		
L1 L2 ☐ ☐	Notes:	

Achieve 9 Chips in the Scoring Zone

Equipment: Wedges, 3 balls, workbook, pen

- Choose a hole that's between 10 and 20 yards away from you. If more than one hole is available, use two or three.

- Scatter 3 balls on fairway grass.

- Play every ball as it lies.

- Before every shot, choose a small, precise landing spot. If you struggle to visualise one, decide where you want the ball to land and place a coin on that spot so you have a target to aim at.

- Move around the green and alternate between holes.

- Based on your skill level, choose a scoring zone of 3ft, 6ft or your average proximity to the hole. The target size should be challenging but achievable.

- Mark the scorecard every time a ball finishes inside the scoring zone with the number of shot attempts it has taken.

- How many shots does it take to achieve 9 shots inside the scoring zone?

- Record your scores and next time aim to complete the practice in one shot less. Every time you set a new personal best, write it down. Be proud of your progress and celebrate your success!

- Aim to reduce the size of the scoring zone over time.

PB Date:							
Total							
PB Date:							
Total							

Achieve 9 Chips in the Scoring Zone

Date	1	2	3	4	5	6	7	8	9	Tot.
Date:										
Target Size:	Notes:									
Date:										
Target Size:	Notes:									
Date:										
Target Size:	Notes:									
Date:										
Target Size:	Notes:									
Date:										
Target Size:	Notes:									
Date:										
Target Size:	Notes:									
Date:										
Target Size:	Notes:									

Achieve 9 Chips in the Scoring Zone										
Date	**1**	**2**	**3**	**4**	**5**	**6**	**7**	**8**	**9**	**Tot.**
Date:										
Target Size:	Notes:									
Date:										
Target Size:	Notes:									
Date:										
Target Size:	Notes:									
Date:										
Target Size:	Notes:									
Date:										
Target Size:	Notes:									
Date:										
Target Size:	Notes:									
Date:										
Target Size:	Notes:									

Dr Nicky Lumb

Achieve 9 Chips in the Scoring Zone										
Date	1	2	3	4	5	6	7	8	9	Tot.
Date:										
Target Size:	Notes:									
Date:										
Target Size:	Notes:									
Date:										
Target Size:	Notes:									
Date:										
Target Size:	Notes:									
Date:										
Target Size:	Notes:									
Date:										
Target Size:	Notes:									
Date:										
Target Size:	Notes:									

Achieve 9 Chips in the Scoring Zone										
Date	1	2	3	4	5	6	7	8	9	Tot.
Date:										
Target Size:	Notes:									
Date:										
Target Size:	Notes:									
Date:										
Target Size:	Notes:									
Date:										
Target Size:	Notes:									
Date:										
Target Size:	Notes:									
Date:										
Target Size:	Notes:									
Date:										
Target Size:	Notes:									

Dr Nicky Lumb

Achieve 9 Chips in the Scoring Zone										
Date	1	2	3	4	5	6	7	8	9	Tot.
Date:										
Target Size:	Notes:									
Date:										
Target Size:	Notes:									
Date:										
Target Size:	Notes:									
Date:										
Target Size:	Notes:									
Date:										
Target Size:	Notes:									
Date:										
Target Size:	Notes:									
Date:										
Target Size:	Notes:									

Jumping Up and Running Down the Ladder

This practice will develop your ability to land a ball on your intended spot as well as your distance control.

Equipment: Wedges, balls, workbook, pen

Jumping Up the Ladder

- Use a flag or marker at 30 yards as your aim line.

- Place a marker in line with the flag at 5 yards.

- Hit from fairway grass.

- Hit the first ball to the 5-yard marker.

- The goal is to get each ball to finish just past the previous one.

- If any ball finishes short or level with the previous ball, that round is over.

- Your Jumping Up the Ladder score is the number of consecutive shots you can get in between 5 and 30 yards before any ball travels less distance than the previous shot.

- Complete the scorecard.

Running Down the Ladder

- Hit the first shot to the flag at 30 yards.

- The goal is to get each ball to finish just short of the previous one.

- If any ball passes or finishes level with the previous ball, that round is over.

- Your score is the number of consecutive shots you hit between 30 and 5 yards before any ball travels further than the previous one.

- Repeat both exercises 3 times.

- Record your best score and next time aim to get one more ball inside the space. Every time you set a new personal best, write it down. Be proud of your progress and celebrate your success!

PB Date:							
Up Ladder							
Down Ladder							
Total							

PB Date:							
Up Ladder							
Down Ladder							
Total							

Up and Down the Ladder						
	Dist	Shot	Dist	Shot	Dist	Shot	*Notes*
Date:	*1*		*2*		*3*		Notes:
Up Ladder							
Down Ladder							
Total							
Date:	*1*		*2*		*3*		Notes:
Up Ladder							
Down Ladder							
Total							

Up and Down the Ladder						
	Dist	Shot	Dist	Shot	Dist	Shot	Notes
Date:	1		2		3		Notes:
Up Ladder							
Down Ladder							
Total							
Date:	1		2		3		Notes:
Up Ladder							
Down Ladder							
Total							
Date:	1		2		3		Notes:
Up Ladder							
Down Ladder							
Total							
Date:	1		2		3		Notes:
Up Ladder							
Down Ladder							
Total							
Date:	1		2		3		Notes:
Up Ladder							
Down Ladder							
Total							
Date:	1		2		3		Notes:
Up Ladder							
Down Ladder							
Total							

Up and Down the Ladder						
	Dist	Shot	Dist	Shot	Dist	Shot	Notes
Date:	1		2		3		Notes:
Up Ladder							
Down Ladder							
Total							
Date:	1		2		3		Notes:
Up Ladder							
Down Ladder							
Total							
Date:	1		2		3		Notes:
Up Ladder							
Down Ladder							
Total							
Date:	1		2		3		Notes:
Up Ladder							
Down Ladder							
Total							
Date:	1		2		3		Notes:
Up Ladder							
Down Ladder							
Total							
Date:	1		2		3		Notes:
Up Ladder							
Down Ladder							
Total							

Up and Down the Ladder

	Dist	Shot	Dist	Shot	Dist	Shot	Notes
Date:	1		2		3		Notes:
Up Ladder							
Down Ladder							
Total							
Date:	1		2		3		Notes:
Up Ladder							
Down Ladder							
Total							
Date:	1		2		3		Notes:
Up Ladder							
Down Ladder							
Total							
Date:	1		2		3		Notes:
Up Ladder							
Down Ladder							
Total							
Date:	1		2		3		Notes:
Up Ladder							
Down Ladder							
Total							
Date:	1		2		3		Notes:
Up Ladder							
Down Ladder							
Total							

Up and Down the Ladder

	Dist	Shot	Dist	Shot	Dist	Shot	Notes
Date:	1		2		3		Notes:
Up Ladder							
Down Ladder							
Total							
Date:	1		2		3		Notes:
Up Ladder							
Down Ladder							
Total							
Date:	1		2		3		Notes:
Up Ladder							
Down Ladder							
Total							
Date:	1		2		3		Notes:
Up Ladder							
Down Ladder							
Total							
Date:	1		2		3		Notes:
Up Ladder							
Down Ladder							
Total							
Date:	1		2		3		Notes:
Up Ladder							
Down Ladder							
Total							

Short, Middle and Long

On the course some shots will be straight forward with plenty of green to work with. Others will be much harder with carries over sand and holes in tight positions with little green to work with. In these situations, a more lofted lob shot will be needed so that the ball flies higher and stops quicker. This is one of the hardest practices in this workbook. It is designed to help you to develop all of your shot making skills and better prepare you for every situation on the course.

Equipment: Wedges, balls, tees, workbook, pen

Level 1

- Choose a hole between 10 and 30 yards.

- Visualise 3 different landing spots to the same hole; short (chip and run), middle and long (lob shot). On the far landing spot, imagine you have to carry the ball over a bunker.

- Place a coin on each landing spot.

- Choose a landing and scoring zone size of 3ft or 6ft. Use your judgement or place tees at that distance at 12, 3, 6 and 9 o'clock around each coin and the hole.

- How many shots does it take to land:

    ○ 3 balls inside the short landing zone and finish in the scoring zone?

    ○ 3 balls inside the middle landing zone and finish in the scoring zone?

    ○ 3 balls inside the long landing zone and finish in the scoring zone?

- Mark the scorecard after every successful shot with the number of shot attempts it has taken.

Dr Nicky Lumb

- Record your scores and next time aim to complete the practice in one shot less. Every time you set a new personal best, write it down. Be proud of your progress and celebrate your success.

Level 2

- How many shots does it take to land:
    - 1 ball inside the short landing zone and finish in the scoring zone?
    - 1 ball inside the middle landing zone and finish in the scoring zone?
    - 1 ball inside the long landing zone and finish in the scoring zone?
- Continue this process until you have hit 3 balls inside each scoring zone.
- Mark the scorecard after every successful shot with the number of shot attempts it has taken.

Record your scores and next time aim to complete the practice in one shot less. Every time you set a new personal best, write it down. Be proud of your progress and celebrate your success.

PB Date:							
Level 1							
PB Date:							
Level 1							
PB Date:							
Level 2							
PB Date:							
Level 2							

Short, Middle and Long										
Date	**1**	**2**	**3**	**4**	**5**	**6**	**7**	**8**	**9**	**Tot.**
Date:										
L1 L2 ☐ ☐	Notes:									
Date:										
L1 L2 ☐ ☐	Notes:									
Date:										
L1 L2 ☐ ☐	Notes:									
Date:										
L1 L2 ☐ ☐	Notes:									
Date:										
L1 L2 ☐ ☐	Notes:									
Date:										
L1 L2 ☐ ☐	Notes:									
Date:										
L1 L2 ☐ ☐	Notes:									
Date:										
L1 L2 ☐ ☐	Notes:									

Dr Nicky Lumb

Short, Middle and Long

Date	1	2	3	4	5	6	7	8	9	Tot.
Date:										
L1 ☐ L2 ☐	Notes:									
Date:										
L1 ☐ L2 ☐	Notes:									
Date:										
L1 ☐ L2 ☐	Notes:									
Date:										
L1 ☐ L2 ☐	Notes:									
Date:										
L1 ☐ L2 ☐	Notes:									
Date:										
L1 ☐ L2 ☐	Notes:									
Date:										
L1 ☐ L2 ☐	Notes:									
Date:										
L1 ☐ L2 ☐	Notes:									

Short, Middle and Long										
Date	1	2	3	4	5	6	7	8	9	Tot.
Date:										
L1 L2 ☐ ☐	Notes:									
Date:										
L1 L2 ☐ ☐	Notes:									
Date:										
L1 L2 ☐ ☐	Notes:									
Date:										
L1 L2 ☐ ☐	Notes:									
Date:										
L1 L2 ☐ ☐	Notes:									
Date:										
L1 L2 ☐ ☐	Notes:									
Date:										
L1 L2 ☐ ☐	Notes:									
Date:										
L1 L2 ☐ ☐	Notes:									

Dr Nicky Lumb

Short, Middle and Long										
Date	**1**	**2**	**3**	**4**	**5**	**6**	**7**	**8**	**9**	**Tot.**
Date:										
L1 L2 ☐ ☐	Notes:									
Date:										
L1 L2 ☐ ☐	Notes:									
Date:										
L1 L2 ☐ ☐	Notes:									
Date:										
L1 L2 ☐ ☐	Notes:									
Date:										
L1 L2 ☐ ☐	Notes:									
Date:										
L1 L2 ☐ ☐	Notes:									
Date:										
L1 L2 ☐ ☐	Notes:									
Date:										
L1 L2 ☐ ☐	Notes:									

Sand Landing Spots

Equipment: Wedges, balls, 4 tees, workbook, pen

- Choose a hole within 10 yards of a bunker.

- Based on your skill level, put tees at 12, 3, 6 and 9 o'clock 6ft, 10ft or your average proximity around the hole.

- From different positions in the bunker, aim to land each ball in the hole.

- Before every shot, visualise the ball landing in the hole.

- How many shots does it take to land 3 balls inside the marked area?

- Complete the scorecard.

- Note how far each ball rolls once it has landed. This will help you determine where shots need to land to reach targets in the future.

- Repeat between 10-20 yards and 20-30 yards.

- Record your scores and next time aim to land 3 balls in each scoring zone in one shot less. Every time you set a new personal best, write it down. Be proud of your progress and celebrate your success!

- Aim to gradually reduce the size of the scoring zone over time.

PB Date:						
Total Shots						
PB Date:						
Total Shots						

Sand Landing Spots				
Date	**Distance**	**< 10yds**	**10-20yds**	**20-30yds**
Date:	Target Size			
	No. of Shots			
Notes:				Total Shots
Date:	Target Size			
	No. of Shots			
Notes:				Total Shots
Date:	Target Size			
	No. of Shots			
Notes:				Total Shots
Date:	Target Size			
	No. of Shots			
Notes:				Total Shots
Date:	Target Size			
	No. of Shots			
Notes:				Total Shots
Date:	Target Size			
	No. of Shots			
Notes:				Total Shots

Sand Landing Spots				
Date	**Distance**	**< 10yds**	**10-20yds**	**20-30yds**
Date:	Target Size			
	No. of Shots			
Notes:				Total Shots
Date:	Target Size			
	No. of Shots			
Notes:				Total Shots
Date:	Target Size			
	No. of Shots			
Notes:				Total Shots
Date:	Target Size			
	No. of Shots			
Notes:				Total Shots
Date:	Target Size			
	No. of Shots			
Notes:				Total Shots
Date:	Target Size			
	No. of Shots			
Notes:				Total Shots

Sand Landing Spots				
Date	**Distance**	**< 10yds**	**10-20yds**	**20-30yds**
Date:	Target Size			
	No. of Shots			
Notes:				Total Shots
Date:	Target Size			
	No. of Shots			
Notes:				Total Shots
Date:	Target Size			
	No. of Shots			
Notes:				Total Shots
Date:	Target Size			
	No. of Shots			
Notes:				Total Shots
Date:	Target Size			
	No. of Shots			
Notes:				Total Shots
Date:	Target Size			
	No. of Shots			
Notes:				Total Shots

Sand Landing Spots				
Date	**Distance**	**< 10yds**	**10-20yds**	**20-30yds**
Date:	Target Size			
	No. of Shots			
Notes:				Total Shots
Date:	Target Size			
	No. of Shots			
Notes:				Total Shots
Date:	Target Size			
	No. of Shots			
Notes:				Total Shots
Date:	Target Size			
	No. of Shots			
Notes:				Total Shots
Date:	Target Size			
	No. of Shots			
Notes:				Total Shots
Date:	Target Size			
	No. of Shots			
Notes:				Total Shots

Dr Nicky Lumb

Sand Landing Spots				
Date	**Distance**	**< 10yds**	**10-20yds**	**20-30yds**
Date:	Target Size			
	No. of Shots			
Notes:				Total Shots
Date:	Target Size			
	No. of Shots			
Notes:				Total Shots
Date:	Target Size			
	No. of Shots			
Notes:				Total Shots
Date:	Target Size			
	No. of Shots			
Notes:				Total Shots
Date:	Target Size			
	No. of Shots			
Notes:				Total Shots
Date:	Target Size			
	No. of Shots			
Notes:				Total Shots

Achieve 9 Sand Shots in the Scoring Zone

Equipment: Wedges, 5 balls, workbook, pen

- Choose a hole within 20 yards. If more than one hole is available, use two or three.

- Scatter 5 balls and use good lies.

- Before every shot, choose a small, precise landing spot. If you struggle to visualise one, decide where you want the ball to land and place a coin or scorecard on that spot so you have a target to aim at.

- Alternate between holes if it is possible.

- Based on your skill level, choose a scoring zone of 6ft, 10ft or your average proximity to the hole. The target size should be challenging but achievable.

- How many shots does it take to achieve 9 shots inside the scoring zone?

- Mark the scorecard after every successful shot with the number of shot attempts it has taken.

- Record your scores and next time aim to complete the practice in one shot less. Every time you set a new personal best, write it down. Be proud of your progress and celebrate your success!

- Aim to reduce the size of the scoring zone over time.

PB Date:						
Total Shots						
PB Date:						
Total Shots						

Dr Nicky Lumb

Achieve 9 Sand Shots in the Scoring Zone

Date	1	2	3	4	5	6	7	8	9	Tot.
Date:										
Target Size:	Notes:									
Date:										
Target Size:	Notes:									
Date:										
Target Size:	Notes:									
Date:										
Target Size:	Notes:									
Date:										
Target Size:	Notes:									
Date:										
Target Size:	Notes:									
Date:										
Target Size:	Notes:									
Date:										
Target Size:	Notes:									

Achieve 9 Sand Shots in the Scoring Zone										
Date	1	2	3	4	5	6	7	8	9	Tot.
Date:										
Target Size:	Notes:									
Date:										
Target Size:	Notes:									
Date:										
Target Size:	Notes:									
Date:										
Target Size:	Notes:									
Date:										
Target Size:	Notes:									
Date:										
Target Size:	Notes:									
Date:										
Target Size:	Notes:									
Date:										
Target Size:	Notes:									

Dr Nicky Lumb

Achieve 9 Sand Shots in the Scoring Zone										
Date	1	2	3	4	5	6	7	8	9	Tot.
Date:										
Target Size:	Notes:									
Date:										
Target Size:	Notes:									
Date:										
Target Size:	Notes:									
Date:										
Target Size:	Notes:									
Date:										
Target Size:	Notes:									
Date:										
Target Size:	Notes:									
Date:										
Target Size:	Notes:									
Date:										
Target Size:	Notes:									

TOURNAMENT PRACTICES

Every shot in this section is unique. To turn any practice into a more challenging tournament practice, hit a full shot or make a full shot practice swing before playing every chip shot so that you replicate what you do before every short game shot on the course.

How Many Shots to Achieve 9 Up and Downs?

Equipment: Wedges, ball, putter, workbook, pen

- Use one ball.

- Each hole is a par 2, 10 to 20 yards long.

- Move around the green and use different flags.

- Include fairway, semi-rough, rough and sand lies. Use different slopes (uphill and downhill lies, ball above and below feet).

- Always choose a small, precise landing spot, and picture how you want the ball to reach the hole. If you struggle to visualise a landing spot, chose one and place a coin on it so you have a target to aim at.

- Before every shot, go through your pre-shot routine.

- Always hole out.

- How many holes does it take to achieve 9 up and downs?

- Mark the scorecard after every successful shot with the number of shot attempts it has taken.

- Put yourself under pressure by setting a target for the number of holes you have to complete the practice. If it takes more, give yourself one opportunity to get up and down from 20-yards, with a consequence of repeating the practice or choosing an unwelcome penalty.

- Record your score and next time aim to complete the practice in one shot less. Every time you set a new personal best, write it down. Be proud of your progress and celebrate your success!

PB Date:							
Total Shots							
PB Date:							
Total Shots							

How Many Shots to Achieve 9 Up and Downs?										
Date	1	2	3	4	5	6	7	8	9	Tot.
Date:										
Notes:										
Date:										
Notes:										
Date:										
Notes:										
Date:										
Notes:										

How Many Shots to Achieve 9 Up and Downs?										
Date	**1**	**2**	**3**	**4**	**5**	**6**	**7**	**8**	**9**	**Tot.**
Date:										
Notes:										
Date:										
Notes:										
Date:										
Notes:										
Date:										
Notes:										
Date:										
Notes:										
Date:										
Notes:										
Date:										
Notes:										
Date:										
Notes:										

How Many Shots to Achieve 9 Up and Downs?

Date	1	2	3	4	5	6	7	8	9	Tot.
Date:										
Notes:										
Date:										
Notes:										
Date:										
Notes:										
Date:										
Notes:										
Date:										
Notes:										
Date:										
Notes:										
Date:										
Notes:										
Date:										
Notes:										

How Many Shots to Achieve 9 Up and Downs?										
Date	**1**	**2**	**3**	**4**	**5**	**6**	**7**	**8**	**9**	**Tot.**
Date:										
Notes:										
Date:										
Notes:										
Date:										
Notes:										
Date:										
Notes:										
Date:										
Notes:										
Date:										
Notes:										
Date:										
Notes:										
Date:										
Notes:										

How Many Shots to Achieve 9 Up and Downs?										
Date	1	2	3	4	5	6	7	8	9	Tot.
Date:										
Notes:										
Date:										
Notes:										
Date:										
Notes:										
Date:										
Notes:										
Date:										
Notes:										
Date:										
Notes:										
Date:										
Notes:										
Date:										
Notes:										

Par 18

The goal of Par 18 is to get up and down in as few shots as possible.

Equipment: Wedges, ball, putter, workbook, pen

Level 1

- With 1 ball, play 9 holes.

- Each hole is a par 2, 10 to 30 yards long.

- Throw each ball to a random spot on fairway grass and play it as it lies.

- Move around the green and use different flags.

- Always choose a small, precise landing spot, and picture how you want the ball to reach the hole. If you struggle to visualise a landing spot, chose one and place a coin on it so you have a target to aim at.

- Before every shot, go through your pre-shot routine.

- Always hole out.

- Scoring: 1 shot = -1, 2 shots = 0, 3 shots = +1, 4 shots = +2.

Level 2

- Repeat Level 1 but play 3 shots from fairway grass, 3 shots from the rough and 3 shots from sand.

- Include different slopes and lies (uphill and downhill lies, ball above and below feet).

- To introduce pressure, set a target score. If you do not reach it, give yourself one opportunity to get up and down from 15yds, with a consequence of repeating the practice or choosing an unwelcome penalty.

Record your scores and next time aim to complete the practice in one shot less. Every time you set a new personal best, write it down. Be proud of your progress and celebrate your success!

PB Date:								
Level 1								
PB Date:								
Level 2								
PB Date:								
Level 2								

Par 18											
Date	1	2	3	4	5	6	7	8	9	Tot.
Date:										
L1 L2 ☐ ☐	Notes:										
Date:										
L1 L2 ☐ ☐	Notes:										
Date:										
L1 L2 ☐ ☐	Notes:										

Par 18										
Date	*1*	*2*	*3*	*4*	*5*	*6*	*7*	*8*	*9*	*Tot.*
Date:										
L1 L2 ☐ ☐	Notes:									
Date:										
L1 L2 ☐ ☐	Notes:									
Date:										
L1 L2 ☐ ☐	Notes:									
Date:										
L1 L2 ☐ ☐	Notes:									
Date:										
L1 L2 ☐ ☐	Notes:									
Date:										
L1 L2 ☐ ☐	Notes:									
Date:										
L1 L2 ☐ ☐	Notes:									
Date:										
L1 L2 ☐ ☐	Notes:									

Dr Nicky Lumb

Par 18										
Date	**1**	**2**	**3**	**4**	**5**	**6**	**7**	**8**	**9**	**Tot.**

Date:

L1 L2
☐ ☐   Notes:

Date:

L1 L2
☐ ☐   Notes:

Date:

L1 L2
☐ ☐   Notes:

Date:

L1 L2
☐ ☐   Notes:

Date:

L1 L2
☐ ☐   Notes:

Date:

L1 L2
☐ ☐   Notes:

Date:

L1 L2
☐ ☐   Notes:

Date:

L1 L2
☐ ☐   Notes:

Par 18									
Date	**1**	**2**	**3**	**4**	**5**	**6**	**7**	**8**	**9**	**Tot.**
Date:										
L1 ☐ L2 ☐	Notes:									
Date:										
L1 ☐ L2 ☐	Notes:									
Date:										
L1 ☐ L2 ☐	Notes:									
Date:										
L1 ☐ L2 ☐	Notes:									
Date:										
L1 ☐ L2 ☐	Notes:									
Date:										
L1 ☐ L2 ☐	Notes:									
Date:										
L1 ☐ L2 ☐	Notes:									
Date:										
L1 ☐ L2 ☐	Notes:									

Dr Nicky Lumb

Par 18										
Date	*1*	*2*	*3*	*4*	*5*	*6*	*7*	*8*	*9*	*Tot.*
Date:										
L1 □ L2 □	Notes:									
Date:										
L1 □ L2 □	Notes:									
Date:										
L1 □ L2 □	Notes:									
Date:										
L1 □ L2 □	Notes:									
Date:										
L1 □ L2 □	Notes:									
Date:										
L1 □ L2 □	Notes:									
Date:										
L1 □ L2 □	Notes:									
Date:										
L1 □ L2 □	Notes:									

ON THE COURSE

With every practice in this section, if a course is busy and you are unable to follow the practice precisely, adapt it by using less balls or alternate the holes you apply the practice on so that you don't delay play!

With every practice, always hole out. You have to do this in every stroke-play competition, so it is beneficial to do it in practice as well.

One Ball Chipping Challenge

- On every hole, play one ball to completion from any distance between 10 and 20 yards from the hole.

- Each hole is a par 2.

- Throw each ball to a random spot and play it as it lies.

- Always choose a small, precise landing spot, and picture how you want the ball to reach the hole.

- Before every shot, go through your pre-shot routine.

- Always hole out.

- Scoring: 1 shot = -1, 2 shots = 0, 3 shots = +1, 4 shots = +2.

- To introduce pressure, set a target score. If you do not reach it, give yourself one opportunity to get up and down from 15 yards, with a consequence of repeating the practice or choosing an unwelcome penalty.

- Record your scores and next time aim to complete the practice in one shot less. Every time you set a new personal best, write it down. Be proud of your progress and celebrate your success!

Dr Nicky Lumb

PB Date:								
Score								

PB Date:								
Score								

One Ball Chipping Challenge

Date:	1	2	3	4	5	6	7	8	9	Tot.
Holes 1 - 9										
Holes 10 - 18										
Notes:									Final Score	

Date:	1	2	3	4	5	6	7	8	9	Tot.
Holes 1 - 9										
Holes 10 - 18										
Notes:									Final Score	

Date:	1	2	3	4	5	6	7	8	9	Tot.
Holes 1 - 9										
Holes 10 - 18										
Notes:									Final Score	

Date:	1	2	3	4	5	6	7	8	9	Tot.
Holes 1 - 9										
Holes 10 - 18										
Notes:									Final Score	

One Ball Chipping Challenge

Date:	1	2	3	4	5	6	7	8	9	Tot.
Holes 1 - 9										
Holes 10 - 18										
Notes:									Final Score	

Date:	1	2	3	4	5	6	7	8	9	Tot.
Holes 1 - 9										
Holes 10 - 18										
Notes:									Final Score	

Date:	1	2	3	4	5	6	7	8	9	Tot.
Holes 1 - 9										
Holes 10 - 18										
Notes:									Final Score	

Date:	1	2	3	4	5	6	7	8	9	Tot.
Holes 1 - 9										
Holes 10 - 18										
Notes:									Final Score	

Date:	1	2	3	4	5	6	7	8	9	Tot.
Holes 1 - 9										
Holes 10 - 18										
Notes:									Final Score	

Dr Nicky Lumb

One Ball Chipping Challenge

Date:	1	2	3	4	5	6	7	8	9	Tot.
Holes 1 - 9										
Holes 10 - 18										
Notes:									Final Score	

Date:	1	2	3	4	5	6	7	8	9	Tot.
Holes 1 - 9										
Holes 10 - 18										
Notes:									Final Score	

Date:	1	2	3	4	5	6	7	8	9	Tot.
Holes 1 - 9										
Holes 10 - 18										
Notes:									Final Score	

Date:	1	2	3	4	5	6	7	8	9	Tot.
Holes 1 - 9										
Holes 10 - 18										
Notes:									Final Score	

Date:	1	2	3	4	5	6	7	8	9	Tot.
Holes 1 - 9										
Holes 10 - 18										
Notes:									Final Score	

One Ball Chipping Challenge

Date:	1	2	3	4	5	6	7	8	9	Tot.
Holes 1 - 9										
Holes 10 - 18										
Notes:									Final Score	

Date:	1	2	3	4	5	6	7	8	9	Tot.
Holes 1 - 9										
Holes 10 - 18										
Notes:									Final Score	

Date:	1	2	3	4	5	6	7	8	9	Tot.
Holes 1 - 9										
Holes 10 - 18										
Notes:									Final Score	

Date:	1	2	3	4	5	6	7	8	9	Tot.
Holes 1 - 9										
Holes 10 - 18										
Notes:									Final Score	

Date:	1	2	3	4	5	6	7	8	9	Tot.
Holes 1 - 9										
Holes 10 - 18										
Notes:									Final Score	

Dr Nicky Lumb

One Ball Chipping Challenge

Date:	1	2	3	4	5	6	7	8	9	Tot.
Holes 1 - 9										
Holes 10 - 18										
Notes:									Final Score	

Date:	1	2	3	4	5	6	7	8	9	Tot.
Holes 1 - 9										
Holes 10 - 18										
Notes:									Final Score	

Date:	1	2	3	4	5	6	7	8	9	Tot.
Holes 1 - 9										
Holes 10 - 18										
Notes:									Final Score	

Date:	1	2	3	4	5	6	7	8	9	Tot.
Holes 1 - 9										
Holes 10 - 18										
Notes:									Final Score	

Date:	1	2	3	4	5	6	7	8	9	Tot.
Holes 1 - 9										
Holes 10 - 18										
Notes:									Final Score	

Chipping Accuracy Challenge

- On each hole, play one ball from two different positions between 10 and 20 yards from the hole.

- Scoring: Inside 3ft - 2 points. Inside 6ft - 1point.

- To introduce pressure, set a target score. If you do not reach it, give yourself one opportunity to get up and down from 20 yards, with a consequence of repeating the practice or choosing an unwelcome penalty.

- Record your score and next time aim to score more points. Every time you set a new personal best, write it down. Be proud of your progress and celebrate your success!

PB Date:							
Score							

PB Date:							
Score							

Chipping Accuracy Challenge

Date:	1	2	3	4	5	6	7	8	9	Tot.
Holes 1 - 9										
Holes 10 - 18										
Notes:									Final Score	

Date:	1	2	3	4	5	6	7	8	9	Tot.
Holes 1 - 9										
Holes 10 - 18										
Notes:									Final Score	

Dr Nicky Lumb

Chipping Accuracy Challenge

Date:	1	2	3	4	5	6	7	8	9	Tot.
Holes 1 - 9										
Holes 10 - 18										
Notes:									Final Score	

Date:	1	2	3	4	5	6	7	8	9	Tot.
Holes 1 - 9										
Holes 10 - 18										
Notes:									Final Score	

Date:	1	2	3	4	5	6	7	8	9	Tot.
Holes 1 - 9										
Holes 10 - 18										
Notes:									Final Score	

Date:	1	2	3	4	5	6	7	8	9	Tot.
Holes 1 - 9										
Holes 10 - 18										
Notes:									Final Score	

Date:	1	2	3	4	5	6	7	8	9	Tot.
Holes 1 - 9										
Holes 10 - 18										
Notes:									Final Score	

Chipping Accuracy Challenge

Date:	1	2	3	4	5	6	7	8	9	Tot.
Holes 1 - 9										
Holes 10 - 18										
Notes:									Final Score	

Date:	1	2	3	4	5	6	7	8	9	Tot.
Holes 1 - 9										
Holes 10 - 18										
Notes:									Final Score	

Date:	1	2	3	4	5	6	7	8	9	Tot.
Holes 1 - 9										
Holes 10 - 18										
Notes:									Final Score	

Date:	1	2	3	4	5	6	7	8	9	Tot.
Holes 1 - 9										
Holes 10 - 18										
Notes:									Final Score	

Date:	1	2	3	4	5	6	7	8	9	Tot.
Holes 1 - 9										
Holes 10 - 18										
Notes:									Final Score	

Dr Nicky Lumb

Chipping Accuracy Challenge

Date:	1	2	3	4	5	6	7	8	9	Tot.
Holes 1 - 9										
Holes 10 - 18										
Notes:									Final Score	

Date:	1	2	3	4	5	6	7	8	9	Tot.
Holes 1 - 9										
Holes 10 - 18										
Notes:									Final Score	

Date:	1	2	3	4	5	6	7	8	9	Tot.
Holes 1 - 9										
Holes 10 - 18										
Notes:									Final Score	

Date:	1	2	3	4	5	6	7	8	9	Tot.
Holes 1 - 9										
Holes 10 - 18										
Notes:									Final Score	

Date:	1	2	3	4	5	6	7	8	9	Tot.
Holes 1 - 9										
Holes 10 - 18										
Notes:									Final Score	

Chipping Accuracy Challenge

Date:	1	2	3	4	5	6	7	8	9	Tot.
Holes 1 - 9										
Holes 10 - 18										
Notes:									Final Score	

Date:	1	2	3	4	5	6	7	8	9	Tot.
Holes 1 - 9										
Holes 10 - 18										
Notes:									Final Score	

Date:	1	2	3	4	5	6	7	8	9	Tot.
Holes 1 - 9										
Holes 10 - 18										
Notes:									Final Score	

Date:	1	2	3	4	5	6	7	8	9	Tot.
Holes 1 - 9										
Holes 10 - 18										
Notes:									Final Score	

Date:	1	2	3	4	5	6	7	8	9	Tot.
Holes 1 - 9										
Holes 10 - 18										
Notes:									Final Score	

Chipping Accuracy Challenge

Date:	1	2	3	4	5	6	7	8	9	Tot.
Holes 1 - 9										
Holes 10 - 18										
Notes:									Final Score	

Date:	1	2	3	4	5	6	7	8	9	Tot.
Holes 1 - 9										
Holes 10 - 18										
Notes:									Final Score	

Date:	1	2	3	4	5	6	7	8	9	Tot.
Holes 1 - 9										
Holes 10 - 18										
Notes:									Final Score	

Date:	1	2	3	4	5	6	7	8	9	Tot.
Holes 1 - 9										
Holes 10 - 18										
Notes:									Final Score	

Date:	1	2	3	4	5	6	7	8	9	Tot.
Holes 1 - 9										
Holes 10 - 18										
Notes:									Final Score	

PITCHING

Approach Shots to the Green

This section consists of shots between 50 and 125 yards from the green. An approach shot finishing within 10ft of the hole creates a realistic one-putt opportunity, while a shot finishing inside 20ft or 30ft is generally within two-putt range. With shots inside 100 yards a 10ft or 20ft target size is used, while the latter extends to 30ft on aporach shots over 100 yards. If your average proximity to the target is inside 20 or 30ft, you may prefer to use that distance.

For your practice to be most effective, it should be more demanding than playing on the course, so whatever target size you use, make sure it challenges you.

With every practice it's vital to always measure your shot accuracy. Use a distance and accuracy feedback device whenever it's possible. If you are unable to mark out scoring zones, use other targets on the range, objects in the background or your best judgement.

If you like to shape the ball from left to right or right to left, you can incorporate it into any practice.

With every practice, you will get the most benefit if you are alert and fully engaged. To make this more likely, any practice can be completed simultaneously with another, so you may want to incorporate a pitching practice with a putting or driving practice so that you change shot types between shots or sets, and move from a training practice towards a more challenging tournament practice.

Approach Shots with Wedges

On the course, most shots will not match the exact distance you hit one of your clubs, and you will have to improvise.

To give you more options, if you are a right-handed golfer, imagine your left arm relates to a clock face and use it to create four different backswing lengths.

A 7.30 swing would be ¼ of the way back. A 9 o'clock swing would be ½ way back, with your left arm parallel to the ground. A 10.30 swing would be a ¾ swing, and a 12 o'clock swing would be a full swing. If you record your different backswing lengths and play them on a video, you may not be in exactly the clock face positions you feel you are. This doesn't matter; what is important is that you feel you are in these positions, can distinguish between them and can repeat each swing length when you need to.

Once you can create and feel four different backswing lengths, work out your average carry distance and proximity to the target with each wedge and swing length. With a consistent rhythm and tempo, this can be effective with bunker shots as well. You can then become more versatile by making small tweaks to your swing. If a pitching wedge 9 o'clock swing goes 100 yards, and a shot is 95 yards, then you can either choke down on the grip by one inch so the ball goes about five yards shorter or make a slightly shorter backswing. If a shot is 105 yards, you can make your backswing a little longer.

Where Are You Now?

The purpose of practice is to improve your skills and shoot lower scores on the course. To do this, you need to know where you are now so that you always have scores to beat, and can measure and monitor your progress.

Wedge Distances with Different Swings

- Choose a wedge and swing length, e.g. pitching wedge 9 o'clock (½) swing.
- Aim at a target that's out of reach so it acts only as a target line.
- From random positions on fairway-length grass, hit 10 shots to the target using the same swing length.
- For sand shots, play from 10 random positions with good lies.
- Discard any really poor shots by hitting another ball but leave in slight mishits; the 10 shots should represent your average, not your best 10!
- To get a more accurate representation of what your distances will be on the course, take time between each shot to hole a four-foot putt or play a short chip if a putting green is not nearby.
- Measure the carry distance of each ball and enter it on the scorecard.
- Calculate your average distance by dividing your total distance by 10.
- With a launch monitor, the software will usually give you your carry distances and average without needing to do any calculations, which can save a lot of time.
- Repeat with every wedge and swing length. This can take a number of sessions to complete properly.
- Enter the distances into the shot matrix on page 109.

Dr Nicky Lumb

Wedge Distances with Different Swings

Date:	1	2	3	4	5	6	7	8	9	10	Total Dist.	Avg Dist.
Club: Swing Length:												
Club: Swing Length:												
Club: Swing Length:												
Club: Swing Length:												
Club: Swing Length:												
Club: Swing Length:												
Club: Swing Length:												
Club: Swing Length:												
Club: Swing Length:												
Club: Swing Length:												
Club: Swing Length:												
Club: Swing Length:												

Wedge Distances with Different Swings

Date:	1	2	3	4	5	6	7	8	9	10	Total Dist.	Avg Dist.
Club: Swing Length:												
Club: Swing Length:												
Club: Swing Length:												
Club: Swing Length:												
Club: Swing Length:												
Club: Swing Length:												
Club: Swing Length:												
Club: Swing Length:												
Club: Swing Length:												
Club: Swing Length:												
Club: Swing Length:												
Club: Swing Length:												

Dr Nicky Lumb

Wedge Distances with Different Swings

Date:	1	2	3	4	5	6	7	8	9	10	Total Dist.	Avg Dist.
Club: Swing Length:												
Club: Swing Length:												
Club: Swing Length:												
Club: Swing Length:												
Club: Swing Length:												
Club: Swing Length:												
Club: Swing Length:												
Club: Swing Length:												
Club: Swing Length:												
Club: Swing Length:												
Club: Swing Length:												
Club: Swing Length:												

Proximity to the Target (Wedges)

- Set a marker at an average swing length distance.

- From random positions on fairway-length grass, hit 10 shots to the target.

- For sand shots, play from 10 random positions with good lies.

- To get a more accurate representation of what your accuracy will be on the course, take time between each shot to hole a four-foot putt or play a short chip if a putting green is not nearby.

- Enter the distance each ball lands from the target onto the scorecard.

- Calculate your average proximity to the target by dividing your total distance by 10.

- Repeat with every wedge swing length. This can take a number of sessions to complete properly.

- Enter the distances into the shot matrix on page 109.

- With a launch monitor, the software will usually give you all of this information which can save a lot of time.

- 4 scorecards are provided so you can check your proximities regularly.

- Aim to reduce your averages and improve your accuracy over time.

Proximity to the Target (Wedges)

Date:	1	2	3	4	5	6	7	8	9	10	Total Dist.	Avg Dist.
Club: Swing Length:												
Club: Swing Length:												
Club: Swing Length:												
Club: Swing Length:												
Club: Swing Length:												
Club: Swing Length:												
Club: Swing Length:												
Club: Swing Length:												
Club: Swing Length:												
Club: Swing Length:												
Club: Swing Length:												
Club: Swing Length:												

Proximity to the Target (Wedges)												
Date:	1	2	3	4	5	6	7	8	9	10	Total Dist.	Avg Dist.
Club: Swing Length:												
Club: Swing Length:												
Club: Swing Length:												
Club: Swing Length:												
Club: Swing Length:												
Club: Swing Length:												
Club: Swing Length:												
Club: Swing Length:												
Club: Swing Length:												
Club: Swing Length:												
Club: Swing Length:												
Club: Swing Length:												

Proximity to the Target (Wedges)

Date:	1	2	3	4	5	6	7	8	9	10	Total Dist.	Avg Dist.
Club: Swing Length:												
Club: Swing Length:												
Club: Swing Length:												
Club: Swing Length:												
Club: Swing Length:												
Club: Swing Length:												
Club: Swing Length:												
Club: Swing Length:												
Club: Swing Length:												
Club: Swing Length:												
Club: Swing Length:												
Club: Swing Length:												

Proximity to the Target (Wedges)

Date:	1	2	3	4	5	6	7	8	9	10	Total Dist.	Avg Dist.
Club: Swing Length:												
Club: Swing Length:												
Club: Swing Length:												
Club: Swing Length:												
Club: Swing Length:												
Club: Swing Length:												
Club: Swing Length:												
Club: Swing Length:												
Club: Swing Length:												
Club: Swing Length:												
Club: Swing Length:												
Club: Swing Length:												

Dr Nicky Lumb

Matrix

Enter your average carry distance with each club at the top of each cell and your average proximity to the target at the bottom, e.g. Pitching Wedge: average distance 100 yards, average proximity to the target 20 feet. Once the matrix is complete, make a copy and keep it in your pocket for easy access. Laminating it can be helpful for when you play in the rain.

Two wedge matrix charts are provided so you can check your averages and update them regularly. Aim to reduce your average proximities over time.

Club	Full Swing
W	100 20

Date	Wedge	¼ Swing	½ Swing	¾ Swing	Full Swing	Sand	Sand

Date	Wedge	¼ Swing	½ Swing	¾ Swing	Full Swing	Sand	Sand

TRAINING PRACTICES

Wedge Matrix Distances

This practice will improve your accuracy with your wedges and different swing lengths (¼, ½, ¾, full). The goal is to hit 3 shots inside the target zone (10ft or 20ft) with each wedge and swing length. Based on your skill level, choose the most appropriate target size. You can use a custom target zone if your average proximity to the target is inside 20ft and 10ft feels a bit too challenging.

Equipment: Wedges, balls, 8 markers, workbook, pen

Level 1

- Choose a flag or create a target.

- Place markers 10ft, 20ft or your average proximity from the hole around the target at 12, 3, 6, and 9 o'clock.

- Choose a wedge and place markers at your average hitting distance for each swing length. Enter these distances into the top of each cell on the scorecard.

- Using a half or 9 o'clock swing, how many shots does it take to hit 3 balls inside the target zone?

- Using a full or 12 o'clock swing, how many shots does it take to hit 3 balls inside the target zone?

- Using a quarter or 7.30 swing, how many shots does it take to hit 3 balls inside the target zone?

- Using a ¾ or 10.30 swing, how many shots does it take to hit 3 balls inside the target zone?

- Record your scores in the bottom of each cell and next time aim to complete this practice in one shot less. Every time you set a new personal best, write it down. Be proud of your progress and celebrate your success!

- Next time you do this practice, use a different wedge.

Level 2

- Choose a flag or create a target.

- Place markers 10ft or 20ft from the target at 12, 3, 6, and 9 o'clock.

- Choose a wedge and place markers at your average hitting distance for each swing length. Enter these distances onto the top of each cell in the scorecard.

- Using a half or 9 o'clock swing, how many shots does it take to hit 1 ball inside the target zone?

- Using a full or 12 o'clock swing, how many shots does it take to hit 1 ball inside the target zone?

- Using a quarter or 7.30 swing, how many shots does it take to hit 1 ball inside the target zone?

- Using a ¾ or 10.30 swing, how many shots does it take to hit 1 ball inside the target zone?

- Follow this sequence until you have hit 3 balls inside the target zone with each swing length.

- Record your scores in the bottom of each cell and next time aim to complete this practice in one shot less. Every time you set a new personal best, write it down. Be proud of your progress and celebrate your success!

- Next time you do this practice, use a different wedge.

PB Date:							
L1 Wedge							
Total Shots							

PB Date:							
L2 Wedge							
Total Shots							

PB Date:							
L2 Wedge							
Total Shots							

Wedge Matrix Distances				Swing Lengths	
Date	1/4	1/2	3/4	Full	Tot.
Date: Wedge:					
Target Size: L1 ☐ L2 ☐	Notes:				
Date: Wedge:					
Target Size: L1 ☐ L2 ☐	Notes:				
Date: Wedge:					
Target Size: L1 ☐ L2 ☐	Notes:				

Dr Nicky Lumb

Wedge Matrix Distances				Swing Lengths	
Date	1/4	1/2	3/4	Full	Tot.
Date: Wedge:					
Target Size: L1 ☐ L2 ☐	Notes:				
Date: Wedge:					
Target Size: L1 ☐ L2 ☐	Notes:				
Date: Wedge:					
Target Size: L1 ☐ L2 ☐	Notes:				
Date: Wedge:					
Target Size: L1 ☐ L2 ☐	Notes:				
Date: Wedge:					
Target Size: L1 ☐ L2 ☐	Notes:				
Date: Wedge:					
Target Size: L1 ☐ L2 ☐	Notes:				

Wedge Matrix Distances				Swing Lengths	
Date	**1/4**	**1/2**	**3/4**	**Full**	**Tot.**
Date: Wedge:					
Target Size: L1 ☐ L2 ☐	Notes:				
Date: Wedge:					
Target Size: L1 ☐ L2 ☐	Notes:				
Date: Wedge:					
Target Size: L1 ☐ L2 ☐	Notes:				
Date: Wedge:					
Target Size: L1 ☐ L2 ☐	Notes:				
Date: Wedge:					
Target Size: L1 ☐ L2 ☐	Notes:				
Date: Wedge:					
Target Size: L1 ☐ L2 ☐	Notes:				

Dr Nicky Lumb

Wedge Matrix Distances				Swing Lengths	
Date	1/4	1/2	3/4	Full	Tot.
Date: Wedge:					
Target Size: L1 ☐ L2 ☐	Notes:				
Date: Wedge:					
Target Size: L1 ☐ L2 ☐	Notes:				
Date: Wedge:					
Target Size: L1 ☐ L2 ☐	Notes:				
Date: Wedge:					
Target Size: L1 ☐ L2 ☐	Notes:				
Date: Wedge:					
Target Size: L1 ☐ L2 ☐	Notes:				
Date: Wedge:					
Target Size: L1 ☐ L2 ☐	Notes:				

Wedge Matrix Distances				Swing Lengths	
Date	**1/4**	**1/2**	**3/4**	**Full**	**Tot.**
Date: Wedge:					
Target Size:		Notes:			
L1 ☐ L2 ☐					
Date: Wedge:					
Target Size:		Notes:			
L1 ☐ L2 ☐					
Date: Wedge:					
Target Size:		Notes:			
L1 ☐ L2 ☐					
Date: Wedge:					
Target Size:		Notes:			
L1 ☐ L2 ☐					
Date: Wedge:					
Target Size:		Notes:			
L1 ☐ L2 ☐					
Date: Wedge:					
Target Size:		Notes:			
L1 ☐ L2 ☐					

Dr Nicky Lumb

Wedge Matrix Distances				Swing Lengths	
Date	1/4	1/2	3/4	Full	Tot.
Date: Wedge:					
Target Size: L1 ☐ L2 ☐	Notes:				
Date: Wedge:					
Target Size: L1 ☐ L2 ☐	Notes:				
Date: Wedge:					
Target Size: L1 ☐ L2 ☐	Notes:				
Date: Wedge:					
Target Size: L1 ☐ L2 ☐	Notes:				
Date: Wedge:					
Target Size: L1 ☐ L2 ☐	Notes:				
Date: Wedge:					
Target Size: L1 ☐ L2 ☐	Notes:				

Stock vs. Random Moving – 50-100 yards

On the course, most shots will not match the exact distance you hit one of your wedges, and you will have to adjust your swing. Stock vs. Random practices will help to develop your distance and directional control, and better prepare you for these situations. This practice uses your own balls and targets. It focuses on hitting shots from different positions, making it one of the most effective practices in simulating playing golf.

This practice includes two distance bands: 50-75yds and 75-100yds. The stock shots are from more familiar distances: 50, 60, 70, 80, 90 and 100 yards. The random shots can be from any distance between 50 and 100 yards.

This design can be adapted and applied to any yardage bands.

Equipment: Wedges, 18 balls, 14 markers, laser rangefinder, workbook, pen

The Stock vs. Random Practice was originally designed by Dr Dave Alred MBE, co-author of Better Practice Better Golf and author of The Pressure Principle.

Dr Nicky Lumb

Level 1

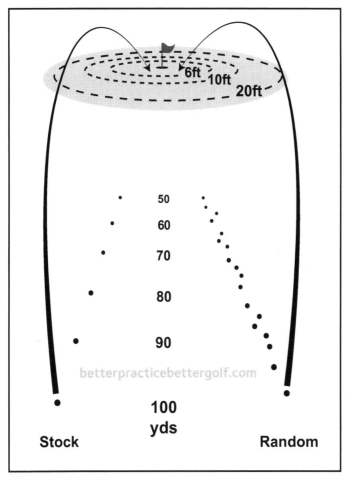

Stock vs. Random Moving Practice

Stock

- Choose a flag or create a target.

- Place markers 10ft and 20ft from the target at 12, 3, 6, and 9 o'clock.

- Put markers at 50, 60, 70, 80, 90 and 100 yards.

- Hit 3 shots from each distance.

- Scoring: Inside 6ft - 3 points. Inside 10ft - 2 points. Inside 20ft - 1 point.

- Complete the scorecard.

- How many points can you score?

- Pick up your balls before hitting the random shots.

Random

- Place 18 balls between the 50- and 100-yard markers so there is one ball every two to three yards.

- In a random order, hit each ball. Aim to have at least a 5-yard gap between each shot.

- Measure the distance of every shot and go through your pre-shot routine.

- Scoring: Inside 6ft - 3 points. Inside 10ft - 2 points. Inside 20ft - 1 point.

- Complete the scorecard

- Can your random score beat your stock score?

- To introduce pressure, set a target score. If you do not reach it, give yourself one opportunity to hit a shot from 70 yards inside 10ft or 20ft, with a consequence of repeating the practice or choosing an unwelcome penalty.

- Record your scores and next time aim to score more points. Every time you set a new personal best, write it down. Be proud of your progress and celebrate your success!

Level 2

Short vs. Long Moving – 50-100 yards

On the course, there will be times when your approach shots into the green must stay short or be past the hole. You will be best prepared if you have practiced these situations before.

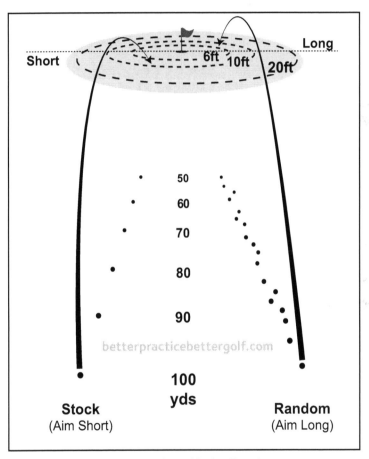

Short vs Long Moving Practice

Stock – Every ball must be short of the target

- Repeat Level 1's method but place markers 10ft and 20ft from the target at 3, 6 and 9 o'clock.

- Every ball must stay short of the target to score.

- Scoring: Short of the target and Inside 6ft - 3 points. Inside 10ft - 2 points. Inside 20ft - 1 point.

Random – Every ball must be past the target

- Place markers 10ft and 20ft from the target at 12, 3 and 9 o'clock.

- Every ball must be past the target to score.

- Scoring: Past the target and Inside: 6ft - 3 points. Inside 10ft - 2 points. Inside 20ft - 1 point.

- To introduce pressure, set a target score. If you do not reach it, give yourself one opportunity to hit a shot from 80 yards short of the target and inside 10ft or 20ft, with a consequence of repeating the practice or choosing an unwelcome penalty.

- Record your scores and next time aim to score more points. Every time you set a new personal best, write it down. Be proud of your progress and celebrate your success!

Level 3

Left vs. Right Moving – 50-100 yards

On the course, there will be times when your approach shots into the green must stay left or right of the hole. You will be best prepared if you have practiced these situations before.

If you like to shape the ball from left to right and right to left, hit every ball that must finish right of the target with a fade and every shot that must finish left with a draw.

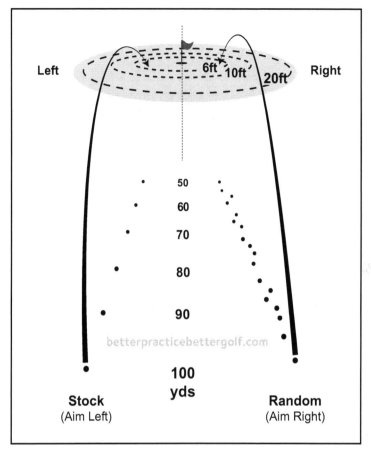

Left vs Right Moving Practice

Stock – Every ball must be left of the target

- Repeat Level 1's method but place markers 10ft and 20ft from the target at 12, 6 and 9 o'clock.

- Every ball must be left of the target to score.

- Scoring: Left of the target and Inside 6ft - 3 points. Inside 10ft - 2 points. Inside 20ft - 1 point.

Random – Every ball must be right of the target

- Place markers 10ft and 20ft from the target at 12, 3 and 6 o'clock.

- Every ball must be right of the target to score.

- Scoring: Right of the target and Inside 6ft - 3 points. Inside 10ft - 2 points. Inside 20ft - 1 point.

- To introduce pressure, set a target score. If you do not reach it, give yourself one opportunity to hit a shot from 90 yards right of the target and inside 10ft or 20ft, with a consequence of repeating the practice or choosing an unwelcome penalty.

- Record your scores and next time aim to score more points. Every time you set a new personal best, write it down. Be proud of your progress and celebrate your success!

PB Date:								
Level:								
PB Date:								
Level:								
PB Date:								
Level:								
PB Date:								
Level:								
PB Date:								
Level:								
PB Date:								
Level:								

Stock vs. Random Moving – 50-100 yards

Scoring: Inside 6ft - 3pts. Inside 10ft - 2 pts. Inside 20ft - 1 pt.

Shots Inside	Stock			Random			Notes
	6ft	10ft	20ft	6ft	10ft	20ft	
Date:							Notes:
L1 ☐ L2 ☐ L3 ☐	Points:			Points:			
Date:							Notes:
L1 ☐ L2 ☐ L3 ☐	Points:			Points:			
Date:							Notes:
L1 ☐ L2 ☐ L3 ☐	Points:			Points:			
Date:							Notes:
L1 ☐ L2 ☐ L3 ☐	Points:			Points:			
Date:							Notes:
L1 ☐ L2 ☐ L3 ☐	Points:			Points:			
Date:							Notes:
L1 ☐ L2 ☐ L3 ☐	Points:			Points:			
Date:							Notes:
L1 ☐ L2 ☐ L3 ☐	Points:			Points:			
Date:							Notes:
L1 ☐ L2 ☐ L3 ☐	Points:			Points:			

Stock vs. Random Moving – 50-100 yards

Scoring: Inside 6ft - 3pts. Inside 10ft - 2 pts. Inside 20ft - 1 pt.

Shots Inside	Stock			Random			Notes
	6ft	10ft	20ft	6ft	10ft	20ft	
Date: L1 ☐ L2 ☐ L3 ☐	Points:			Points:			Notes:
Date: L1 ☐ L2 ☐ L3 ☐	Points:			Points:			Notes:
Date: L1 ☐ L2 ☐ L3 ☐	Points:			Points:			Notes:
Date: L1 ☐ L2 ☐ L3 ☐	Points:			Points:			Notes:
Date: L1 ☐ L2 ☐ L3 ☐	Points:			Points:			Notes:
Date: L1 ☐ L2 ☐ L3 ☐	Points:			Points:			Notes:
Date: L1 ☐ L2 ☐ L3 ☐	Points:			Points:			Notes:
Date: L1 ☐ L2 ☐ L3 ☐	Points:			Points:			Notes:

Dr Nicky Lumb

Stock vs. Random Moving – 50-100 yards

Scoring: Inside 6ft - 3pts. Inside 10ft - 2 pts. Inside 20ft - 1 pt.

Shots Inside	Stock			Random			Notes
	6ft	10ft	20ft	6ft	10ft	20ft	
Date:							Notes:
L1 L2 L3 ☐ ☐ ☐	Points:			Points:			
Date:							Notes:
L1 L2 L3 ☐ ☐ ☐	Points:			Points:			
Date:							Notes:
L1 L2 L3 ☐ ☐ ☐	Points:			Points:			
Date:							Notes:
L1 L2 L3 ☐ ☐ ☐	Points:			Points:			
Date:							Notes:
L1 L2 L3 ☐ ☐ ☐	Points:			Points:			
Date:							Notes:
L1 L2 L3 ☐ ☐ ☐	Points:			Points:			
Date:							Notes:
L1 L2 L3 ☐ ☐ ☐	Points:			Points:			
Date:							Notes:
L1 L2 L3 ☐ ☐ ☐	Points:			Points:			

Stock vs. Random Moving – 50-100 yards							
Scoring: Inside 6ft - 3pts. Inside 10ft - 2 pts. Inside 20ft - 1 pt.							
	Stock			Random			
Shots Inside	6ft	10ft	20ft	6ft	10ft	20ft	Notes
Date:							Notes:
L1 L2 L3 ☐ ☐ ☐	Points:			Points:			
Date:							Notes:
L1 L2 L3 ☐ ☐ ☐	Points:			Points:			
Date:							Notes:
L1 L2 L3 ☐ ☐ ☐	Points:			Points:			
Date:							Notes:
L1 L2 L3 ☐ ☐ ☐	Points:			Points:			
Date:							Notes:
L1 L2 L3 ☐ ☐ ☐	Points:			Points:			
Date:							Notes:
L1 L2 L3 ☐ ☐ ☐	Points:			Points:			
Date:							Notes:
L1 L2 L3 ☐ ☐ ☐	Points:			Points:			
Date:							Notes:
L1 L2 L3 ☐ ☐ ☐	Points:			Points:			

Stock vs. Random Moving – 50-100 yards							
Scoring: Inside 6ft - 3pts. Inside 10ft - 2 pts. Inside 20ft - 1 pt.							
	Stock			Random			
Shots Inside	6ft	10ft	20ft	6ft	10ft	20ft	Notes
Date:							Notes:
L1 L2 L3 ☐ ☐ ☐	Points:			Points:			
Date:							Notes:
L1 L2 L3 ☐ ☐ ☐	Points:			Points:			
Date:							Notes:
L1 L2 L3 ☐ ☐ ☐	Points:			Points:			
Date:							Notes:
L1 L2 L3 ☐ ☐ ☐	Points:			Points:			
Date:							Notes:
L1 L2 L3 ☐ ☐ ☐	Points:			Points:			
Date:							Notes:
L1 L2 L3 ☐ ☐ ☐	Points:			Points:			
Date:							Notes:
L1 L2 L3 ☐ ☐ ☐	Points:			Points:			
Date:							Notes:
L1 L2 L3 ☐ ☐ ☐	Points:			Points:			

Stock vs. Random Moving – 100-125 yards

This practice incorporates one distance band: 100-125yds.

Equipment: Wedges / Short Irons, 18 balls, 14 markers, laser rangefinder, workbook, pen

Stock

- Choose a flag or create a target.
- Place markers 10ft and 30ft from the target at 12, 3, 6 and 9 o'clock.
- Put markers at 100, 105, 110, 115, 120 and 125 yards.
- Hit 3 shots from each distance.
- Scoring: Inside 10ft - 3pts. Inside 20ft - 2 pts. Inside 30ft - 1pt.
- Complete the scorecard. How many points can you score?
- Pick up your balls before hitting the random shots.

Random

- Place 18 balls between the 100- and 125-yard markers so there is one ball every one to two yards.
- In a random order, hit each ball. Aim to have at least a 3-yard gap between each shot.
- Measure the distance of every shot and go through your pre-shot routine.
- Scoring: Inside 10ft - 3pts. Inside 20ft - 2 pts. Inside 30ft - 1pt.
- Can your random score beat your stock score?

- To introduce pressure, set a target score. If you do not reach it, give yourself one opportunity to hit a shot from 110 yards inside 10ft, 20ft or 30ft, with a consequence of repeating the practice or choosing an unwelcome penalty.

- Record your scores and next time aim to score more points. Every time you set a new personal best, write it down. Be proud of your progress and celebrate your success!

PB Date:							
Score							
PB Date:							
Score							

Stock vs. Random Moving – 100-125 yards							
	Stock			Random			
Shots Inside	10ft	20ft	30ft	10ft	20ft	30ft	Notes
Date:							Notes:
Total Points:	Points:			Points:			
Date:							Notes:
Total Points:							
Date:							Notes:
Total Points:							
Date:							Notes:
Total Points:							
Scoring: Inside 10ft - 3 pts. Inside 20ft - 2 pts Inside 30ft - 1 pt							

Stock vs. Random Moving – 100-125 yards

Shots Inside	Stock			Random			Notes
	10ft	20ft	30ft	10ft	20ft	30ft	
Date:							Notes:
Total Points:							
Date:							Notes:
Total Points:							
Date:							Notes:
Total Points:							
Date:							Notes:
Total Points:							
Date:							Notes:
Total Points:							
Date:							Notes:
Total Points:							
Date:							Notes:
Total Points:							
Date:							Notes:
Total Points:							
Date:							Notes:
Total Points:							

Scoring: Inside 10ft - 3 pts. Inside 20ft - 2 pts Inside 30ft - 1 pt

Dr Nicky Lumb

Stock vs. Random Moving – 100-125 yards							
	Stock			Random			
Shots Inside	10ft	20ft	30ft	10ft	20ft	30ft	Notes
Date:							Notes:
Total Points:							
Date:							Notes:
Total Points:							
Date:							Notes:
Total Points:							
Date:							Notes:
Total Points:							
Date:							Notes:
Total Points:							
Date:							Notes:
Total Points:							
Date:							Notes:
Total Points:							
Date:							Notes:
Total Points:							
Date:							Notes:
Total Points:							

Scoring: Inside 10ft - 3 pts. Inside 20ft - 2 pts Inside 30ft - 1 pt

Stock vs. Random Moving – 100-125 yards

Shots Inside	Stock			Random			Notes
	10ft	20ft	30ft	10ft	20ft	30ft	
Date:							Notes:
Total Points:							
Date:							Notes:
Total Points:							
Date:							Notes:
Total Points:							
Date:							Notes:
Total Points:							
Date:							Notes:
Total Points:							
Date:							Notes:
Total Points:							
Date:							Notes:
Total Points:							
Date:							Notes:
Total Points:							
Date:							Notes:
Total Points:							

Scoring: Inside 10ft - 3 pts. Inside 20ft - 2 pts Inside 30ft - 1 pt

Dr Nicky Lumb

Stock vs. Random Moving – 100-125 yards							
	Stock			**Random**			
Shots Inside	**10ft**	**20ft**	**30ft**	**10ft**	**20ft**	**30ft**	**Notes**
Date:							Notes:
Total Points:							
Date:							Notes:
Total Points:							
Date:							Notes:
Total Points:							
Date:							Notes:
Total Points:							
Date:							Notes:
Total Points:							
Date:							Notes:
Total Points:							
Date:							Notes:
Total Points:							
Date:							Notes:
Total Points:							
Date:							Notes:
Total Points:							
Scoring: Inside 10ft - 3 pts. Inside 20ft - 2 pts Inside 30ft - 1 pt							

Stock vs. Random Static – 50-100 yards

On the course, most shots will not match the exact distance you hit one of your wedges and you will have to adjust your swing. Stock vs. Random practices will help to develop your distance and directional control and better prepare you for these situations.

This practice involves hitting shots from a static tee. It's easiest to do it with your own targets but if you are on a driving range, use the most appropriate targets and objects in the background or your best judgement to determine your accuracy.

This practice includes two distance bands: 50-75yds and 75-100yds. The stock shots are from more familiar distances: 50, 60, 70, 80, 90 and 100 yards. The random shots can be from any distance between 50 and 100 yards.

To increase the challenge of this practice, predict if the ball will land inside the scoring zone immediately after hitting each shot. Score how many predictions you get right.

Equipment: Wedges, balls, 8 markers, laser rangefinder, workbook, pen

(Use a launch monitor to receive carry distance and accuracy feedback after every shot if you have access to one).

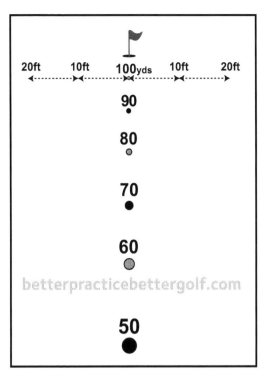

Stock vs. Random Static Practice

Level 1

Stock

- Place markers at 50, 60, 70, 80, 90 and 100 yards in a relatively straight line. It's easiest if you have at least 2 different coloured markers so you can alternate between colours every 10 yards.

- Choose a target size (e.g., 10ft or 20ft). The target size should be challenging but achievable.

- At 100 yards, place markers on either side of the target at that distance so you can judge if each ball lands directionally inside them. There are 10 yards (30ft) between each distance marker to help you judge the distance and if each ball lands inside the target zone, if you are unable to use a distance and accuracy feedback device.

- Hit 3 shots to each target. Continue this process until 9 shots have landed within the target zone.

- Every time a ball lands in the scoring zone, mark the scorecard with the number of shot attempts it has taken.

- How many shots does it take for 9 balls to land in the target zone? Record your stock shot total.

Random

- Use a random number app to generate different numbers between 50 and 100. These will be your shot distances.

- Using the targets in place from the stock shots, use your best judgement to determine your accuracy.

- Go through your pre-shot routine before every shot.

- How many shots does it take for 9 balls to land in the target zone?

- Every time a ball lands in the scoring zone, mark the scorecard with the number of shot attempts it has taken.

- Can your random score beat your stock score?

- Put yourself under pressure by setting a target for the number of attempts you have to complete the practice. If it takes more, give yourself one opportunity to hit a shot within 10ft or 20ft of 100 yards, with a consequence of repeating the practice or choosing an unwelcome penalty.

- Record your scores and next time aim to complete the practice in less shots. Every time you set a new personal best, write it down. Be proud of your progress and celebrate your success!

Level 2

Left vs. Right Static – 50-100 yards

On the course, there will be times when your approach shots into the green must stay left or right of the hole. You will be best prepared if you have practiced these situations before.

If you like to shape the ball, hit every ball that must finish right of the target with a fade, and every shot that must finish left with a draw.

Stock – Every ball must finish left of the target

- Repeat Level 1's method.
- Every ball must be left of the target to score.
- How many shots does it take for 9 balls to land in the target zone? Record your stock shot total.

Random – Every ball must finish right of the target

- Use a random number app to generate different numbers between 50 and 100. These are your shot distances.
- Every ball must be right of the target to score.
- How many shots does it take for 9 balls to land in the target zone?
- Can your random score beat your stock score?
- Put yourself under pressure by setting a target for the number of attempts you have to complete the practice. If it takes more, give yourself one opportunity to hit a shot within 10ft or 20ft of 80 yards and left of it, with a consequence of choosing an unwelcome penalty.
- Record your scores and next time aim to complete the practice in less shots. Every time you set a new personal best, write it down. Be proud of your progress and celebrate your success!

PB Date:								
Level:								

PB Date:								
Level:								

PB Date:								
Level:								

PB Date:								
Level:								

PB Date:								
Level:								

Stock vs. Random Static – 50-100 yards

	1	2	3	4	5	6	7	8	9	Tot.
Stock										
Random										
Date: / Target Size:	Notes: L1 ☐ L2 ☐								Total Shots	
Stock										
Random										
Date: / Target Size:	Notes: L1 ☐ L2 ☐								Total Shots	
Stock										
Random										
Date: / Target Size:	Notes: L1 ☐ L2 ☐								Total Shots	

Dr Nicky Lumb

Stock vs. Random Static – 50-100 yards

	1	2	3	4	5	6	7	8	9	Tot.
Stock										
Random										

Date:	Notes:	Total Shots
Target Size:	L1 ☐ L2 ☐	

	1	2	3	4	5	6	7	8	9	Tot.
Stock										
Random										

Date:	Notes:	Total Shots
Target Size:	L1 ☐ L2 ☐	

	1	2	3	4	5	6	7	8	9	Tot.
Stock										
Random										

Date:	Notes:	Total Shots
Target Size:	L1 ☐ L2 ☐	

	1	2	3	4	5	6	7	8	9	Tot.
Stock										
Random										

Date:	Notes:	Total Shots
Target Size:	L1 ☐ L2 ☐	

	1	2	3	4	5	6	7	8	9	Tot.
Stock										
Random										

Date:	Notes:	Total Shots
Target Size:	L1 ☐ L2 ☐	

	1	2	3	4	5	6	7	8	9	Tot.
Stock										
Random										

Date:	Notes:	Total Shots
Target Size:	L1 ☐ L2 ☐	

Stock vs. Random Static – 50-100 yards

	1	2	3	4	5	6	7	8	9	Tot.
Stock										
Random										

Date:	Notes:	Total Shots
Target Size:	L1 ☐ L2 ☐	

	1	2	3	4	5	6	7	8	9	Tot.
Stock										
Random										

Date:	Notes:	Total Shots
Target Size:	L1 ☐ L2 ☐	

	1	2	3	4	5	6	7	8	9	Tot.
Stock										
Random										

Date:	Notes:	Total Shots
Target Size:	L1 ☐ L2 ☐	

	1	2	3	4	5	6	7	8	9	Tot.
Stock										
Random										

Date:	Notes:	Total Shots
Target Size:	L1 ☐ L2 ☐	

	1	2	3	4	5	6	7	8	9	Tot.
Stock										
Random										

Date:	Notes:	Total Shots
Target Size:	L1 ☐ L2 ☐	

	1	2	3	4	5	6	7	8	9	Tot.
Stock										
Random										

Date:	Notes:	Total Shots
Target Size:	L1 ☐ L2 ☐	

Dr Nicky Lumb

Stock vs. Random Static – 50-100 yards	1	2	3	4	5	6	7	8	9	Tot.
Stock										
Random										

Date:	Notes:	Total Shots
Target Size:	L1 ☐ L2 ☐	

	1	2	3	4	5	6	7	8	9	Tot.
Stock										
Random										

Date:	Notes:	Total Shots
Target Size:	L1 ☐ L2 ☐	

	1	2	3	4	5	6	7	8	9	Tot.
Stock										
Random										

Date:	Notes:	Total Shots
Target Size:	L1 ☐ L2 ☐	

	1	2	3	4	5	6	7	8	9	Tot.
Stock										
Random										

Date:	Notes:	Total Shots
Target Size:	L1 ☐ L2 ☐	

	1	2	3	4	5	6	7	8	9	Tot.
Stock										
Random										

Date:	Notes:	Total Shots
Target Size:	L1 ☐ L2 ☐	

	1	2	3	4	5	6	7	8	9	Tot.
Stock										
Random										

Date:	Notes:	Total Shots
Target Size:	L1 ☐ L2 ☐	

Stock vs. Random Static – 50-100 yards

	1	2	3	4	5	6	7	8	9	Tot.
Stock										
Random										

Date:	Notes:	Total Shots
Target Size:	L1 ☐ L2 ☐	

	1	2	3	4	5	6	7	8	9	Tot.
Stock										
Random										

Date:	Notes:	Total Shots
Target Size:	L1 ☐ L2 ☐	

	1	2	3	4	5	6	7	8	9	Tot.
Stock										
Random										

Date:	Notes:	Total Shots
Target Size:	L1 ☐ L2 ☐	

	1	2	3	4	5	6	7	8	9	Tot.
Stock										
Random										

Date:	Notes:	Total Shots
Target Size:	L1 ☐ L2 ☐	

	1	2	3	4	5	6	7	8	9	Tot.
Stock										
Random										

Date:	Notes:	Total Shots
Target Size:	L1 ☐ L2 ☐	

	1	2	3	4	5	6	7	8	9	Tot.
Stock										
Random										

Date:	Notes:	Total Shots
Target Size:	L1 ☐ L2 ☐	

Dr Nicky Lumb

Stock vs. Random Static – 50-100 yards

	1	2	3	4	5	6	7	8	9	Tot.
Stock										
Random										

| Date: | Notes: | | | | | | | | Total Shots |
| Target Size: | | | | | L1 ☐ | L2 ☐ | | | |

	1	2	3	4	5	6	7	8	9	Tot.
Stock										
Random										

| Date: | Notes: | | | | | | | | Total Shots |
| Target Size: | | | | | L1 ☐ | L2 ☐ | | | |

	1	2	3	4	5	6	7	8	9	Tot.
Stock										
Random										

| Date: | Notes: | | | | | | | | Total Shots |
| Target Size: | | | | | L1 ☐ | L2 ☐ | | | |

	1	2	3	4	5	6	7	8	9	Tot.
Stock										
Random										

| Date: | Notes: | | | | | | | | Total Shots |
| Target Size: | | | | | L1 ☐ | L2 ☐ | | | |

	1	2	3	4	5	6	7	8	9	Tot.
Stock										
Random										

| Date: | Notes: | | | | | | | | Total Shots |
| Target Size: | | | | | L1 ☐ | L2 ☐ | | | |

	1	2	3	4	5	6	7	8	9	Tot.
Stock										
Random										

| Date: | Notes: | | | | | | | | Total Shots |
| Target Size: | | | | | L1 ☐ | L2 ☐ | | | |

Stock vs. Random Static – 100-125 yards

This practice focuses on shots between 100 and 125 yards.

Equipment: Wedges / Short Irons, balls, 8 markers, laser rangefinder, workbook, pen

(Use a launch monitor to receive carry distance and accuracy feedback after every shot if you have access to one).

Stock

- Place markers at 100, 105, 110, 115, 120 and 125 yards in a relatively straight line. It's easiest if you have at least 2 different coloured markers so you can alternate between colours every 5 yards.

- Choose a target size (e.g., 10ft or 30ft). The target size should be challenging but achievable.

- At 125 yards, place markers on either side of the target at that distance so you can judge if each ball lands directionally inside them. There are 5 yards (15ft) between each distance marker to help you judge the distance and if each ball lands inside 10ft or 30ft, if you are unable to use a distance and accuracy feedback device.

- Hit 3 shots to each target. Continue this process until 9 shots have landed within the target zone.

- Every time a ball lands in the scoring zone, mark the scorecard with the number of shot attempts it has taken.

- How many shots does it take for 9 balls to land in the target zone? Record your stock shot total.

- To increase the challenge, predict if each ball will land inside the scoring zone immediately after hitting each shot. Score how many predictions you get right.

Random

- Use a random number app to generate different numbers between 100 and 125. These will be your shot distances.

- Go through your pre-shot routine before every shot.

- How many shots does it take for 9 balls to land in the target zone?

- Every time a ball lands in the scoring zone, mark the scorecard with the number of shot attempts it has taken.

- Can your random score beat your stock score?

- Put yourself under pressure by setting a target for the number of attempts you have to complete the practice. If it takes more, give yourself one opportunity to hit a shot within 10ft or 30ft of 110 yards, with a consequence of repeating the practice or choosing an unwelcome penalty.

- Record your scores and next time aim to complete the practice in less shots. Every time you set a new personal best, write it down. Be proud of your progress and celebrate your success!

PB Date:							
Total Shots							

PB Date:							
Total Shots							

Stock vs. Random Static – 100-125 yards										
	1	*2*	*3*	*4*	*5*	*6*	*7*	*8*	*9*	*Tot.*
Stock										
Random										
Date: Target Size:	Notes:								Total Shots	

Stock vs. Random Static – 100-125 yards

	1	2	3	4	5	6	7	8	9	Tot.
Stock										
Random										

Date:	Notes:	Total Shots
Target Size:		

	1	2	3	4	5	6	7	8	9	Tot.
Stock										
Random										

Date:	Notes:	Total Shots
Target Size:		

	1	2	3	4	5	6	7	8	9	Tot.
Stock										
Random										

Date:	Notes:	Total Shots
Target Size:		

	1	2	3	4	5	6	7	8	9	Tot.
Stock										
Random										

Date:	Notes:	Total Shots
Target Size:		

	1	2	3	4	5	6	7	8	9	Tot.
Stock										
Random										

Date:	Notes:	Total Shots
Target Size:		

	1	2	3	4	5	6	7	8	9	Tot.
Stock										
Random										

Date:	Notes:	Total Shots
Target Size:		

Dr Nicky Lumb

Stock vs. Random Static – 100-125 yards

	1	2	3	4	5	6	7	8	9	Tot.
Stock										
Random										

| Date: | Notes: | | | | | | | | Total Shots | |
| Target Size: | | | | | | | | | | |

	1	2	3	4	5	6	7	8	9	Tot.
Stock										
Random										

| Date: | Notes: | | | | | | | | Total Shots | |
| Target Size: | | | | | | | | | | |

| Stock | | | | | | | | | | |
| Random | | | | | | | | | | |

| Date: | Notes: | | | | | | | | Total Shots | |
| Target Size: | | | | | | | | | | |

| Stock | | | | | | | | | | |
| Random | | | | | | | | | | |

| Date: | Notes: | | | | | | | | Total Shots | |
| Target Size: | | | | | | | | | | |

| Stock | | | | | | | | | | |
| Random | | | | | | | | | | |

| Date: | Notes: | | | | | | | | Total Shots | |
| Target Size: | | | | | | | | | | |

| Stock | | | | | | | | | | |
| Random | | | | | | | | | | |

| Date: | Notes: | | | | | | | | Total Shots | |
| Target Size: | | | | | | | | | | |

Stock vs. Random Static – 100-125 yards

	1	2	3	4	5	6	7	8	9	Tot.
Stock										
Random										

Date:	Notes:	Total Shots
Target Size:		

	1	2	3	4	5	6	7	8	9	Tot.
Stock										
Random										

Date:	Notes:	Total Shots
Target Size:		

	1	2	3	4	5	6	7	8	9	Tot.
Stock										
Random										

Date:	Notes:	Total Shots
Target Size:		

	1	2	3	4	5	6	7	8	9	Tot.
Stock										
Random										

Date:	Notes:	Total Shots
Target Size:		

	1	2	3	4	5	6	7	8	9	Tot.
Stock										
Random										

Date:	Notes:	Total Shots
Target Size:		

	1	2	3	4	5	6	7	8	9	Tot.
Stock										
Random										

Date:	Notes:	Total Shots
Target Size:		

Dr Nicky Lumb

Stock vs. Random Static – 100-125 yards

	1	2	3	4	5	6	7	8	9	Tot.
Stock										
Random										

Date:	Notes:	Total Shots
Target Size:		

	1	2	3	4	5	6	7	8	9	Tot.
Stock										
Random										

Date:	Notes:	Total Shots
Target Size:		

	1	2	3	4	5	6	7	8	9	Tot.
Stock										
Random										

Date:	Notes:	Total Shots
Target Size:		

	1	2	3	4	5	6	7	8	9	Tot.
Stock										
Random										

Date:	Notes:	Total Shots
Target Size:		

	1	2	3	4	5	6	7	8	9	Tot.
Stock										
Random										

Date:	Notes:	Total Shots
Target Size:		

	1	2	3	4	5	6	7	8	9	Tot.
Stock										
Random										

Date:	Notes:	Total Shots
Target Size:		

TOURNAMENT PRACTICES

ON THE COURSE

With every practice in this section, if a course is busy and you are unable to follow the practice precisely, adapt it by using less balls or alternate the holes you apply the practice on so that you don't delay play!

With every practice, always hole out. You have to do this in every stroke-play competition, so it is beneficial to do it in practice as well.

One Ball Pitching Challenge

- On every hole, play an extra ball to completion from the distances on the scorecard.

- Every hole is a par 3.

- Fill in the scorecard.

- To introduce pressure, set a target score. If you do not reach it, give yourself one opportunity to hole out in three shots or less from 90 yards, with a consequence of repeating the practice or choosing an unwelcome penalty.

- Record your total score and next time aim to be one shot better. Every time you set a new personal best, write it down. Be proud of your progress and celebrate your success!

PB Date:							
Score							
PB Date:							
Score							

One Ball Pitching Challenge

Date:	50	60	70	80	90	100	50	60	70	Tot.
Holes 1 - 9										
Holes 10 - 18										
Notes:									Final Score	

Date:	50	60	70	80	90	100	50	60	70	Tot.
Holes 1 - 9										
Holes 10 - 18										
Notes:									Final Score	

Date:	50	60	70	80	90	100	50	60	70	Tot.
Holes 1 - 9										
Holes 10 - 18										
Notes:									Final Score	

Date:	50	60	70	80	90	100	50	60	70	Tot.
Holes 1 - 9										
Holes 10 - 18										
Notes:									Final Score	

Date:	50	60	70	80	90	100	50	60	70	Tot.
Holes 1 - 9										
Holes 10 - 18										
Notes:									Final Score	

One Ball Pitching Challenge

Date:	50	60	70	80	90	100	50	60	70	Tot.
Holes 1 - 9										
Holes 10 - 18										
Notes:									Final Score	

Date:	50	60	70	80	90	100	50	60	70	Tot.
Holes 1 - 9										
Holes 10 - 18										
Notes:									Final Score	

Date:	50	60	70	80	90	100	50	60	70	Tot.
Holes 1 - 9										
Holes 10 - 18										
Notes:									Final Score	

Date:	50	60	70	80	90	100	50	60	70	Tot.
Holes 1 - 9										
Holes 10 - 18										
Notes:									Final Score	

Date:	50	60	70	80	90	100	50	60	70	Tot.
Holes 1 - 9										
Holes 10 - 18										
Notes:									Final Score	

Dr Nicky Lumb

One Ball Pitching Challenge

Date:	50	60	70	80	90	100	50	60	70	Tot.
Holes 1 - 9										
Holes 10 - 18										
Notes:									Final Score	

Date:	50	60	70	80	90	100	50	60	70	Tot.
Holes 1 - 9										
Holes 10 - 18										
Notes:									Final Score	

Date:	50	60	70	80	90	100	50	60	70	Tot.
Holes 1 - 9										
Holes 10 - 18										
Notes:									Final Score	

Date:	50	60	70	80	90	100	50	60	70	Tot.
Holes 1 - 9										
Holes 10 - 18										
Notes:									Final Score	

Date:	50	60	70	80	90	100	50	60	70	Tot.
Holes 1 - 9										
Holes 10 - 18										
Notes:									Final Score	

One Ball Pitching Challenge

Date:	50	60	70	80	90	100	50	60	70	Tot.
Holes 1 - 9										
Holes 10 - 18										
Notes:									Final Score	

Date:	50	60	70	80	90	100	50	60	70	Tot.
Holes 1 - 9										
Holes 10 - 18										
Notes:									Final Score	

Date:	50	60	70	80	90	100	50	60	70	Tot.
Holes 1 - 9										
Holes 10 - 18										
Notes:									Final Score	

Date:	50	60	70	80	90	100	50	60	70	Tot.
Holes 1 - 9										
Holes 10 - 18										
Notes:									Final Score	

Date:	50	60	70	80	90	100	50	60	70	Tot.
Holes 1 - 9										
Holes 10 - 18										
Notes:									Final Score	

One Ball Pitching Challenge

Date:	50	60	70	80	90	100	50	60	70	Tot.
Holes 1 - 9										
Holes 10 - 18										
Notes:									Final Score	

Date:	50	60	70	80	90	100	50	60	70	Tot.
Holes 1 - 9										
Holes 10 - 18										
Notes:									Final Score	

Date:	50	60	70	80	90	100	50	60	70	Tot.
Holes 1 - 9										
Holes 10 - 18										
Notes:									Final Score	

Date:	50	60	70	80	90	100	50	60	70	Tot.
Holes 1 - 9										
Holes 10 - 18										
Notes:									Final Score	

Date:	50	60	70	80	90	100	50	60	70	Tot.
Holes 1 - 9										
Holes 10 - 18										
Notes:									Final Score	

Pitching Accuracy Challenge

If a course is busy, you can do this practice with 1 or 2 balls. Please don't delay play!

- On each hole, play 3 balls into the green from the stated distance.

- Scoring: Inside 6ft - 3pts. Inside 10ft - 2pts. Inside 20ft - 1pt.

- To introduce pressure, set a target score. If you do not reach it, give yourself one opportunity to hole out in three shots or less from 100 yards, with a consequence of repeating the practice or choosing an unwelcome penalty.

- Record your score and next time aim to score more points. Every time you set a new personal best, write it down. Be proud of your progress and celebrate your success!

PB Date:							
Score							

PB Date:							
Score							

Pitching Accuracy Challenge										
Date:	50	60	70	80	90	100	50	60	70	Tot.
Holes 1 - 9										
Holes 10 - 18										
Notes:									Final Score	

Pitching Accuracy Challenge

Date:	50	60	70	80	90	100	50	60	70	Tot.
Holes 1 - 9										
Holes 10 - 18										
Notes:								Final Score		

Date:	50	60	70	80	90	100	50	60	70	Tot.
Holes 1 - 9										
Holes 10 - 18										
Notes:								Final Score		

Date:	50	60	70	80	90	100	50	60	70	Tot.
Holes 1 - 9										
Holes 10 - 18										
Notes:								Final Score		

Date:	50	60	70	80	90	100	50	60	70	Tot.
Holes 1 - 9										
Holes 10 - 18										
Notes:								Final Score		

Date:	50	60	70	80	90	100	50	60	70	Tot.
Holes 1 - 9										
Holes 10 - 18										
Notes:								Final Score		

Pitching Accuracy Challenge

Date:	50	60	70	80	90	100	50	60	70	Tot.
Holes 1 - 9										
Holes 10 - 18										
Notes:								Final Score		

Date:	50	60	70	80	90	100	50	60	70	Tot.
Holes 1 - 9										
Holes 10 - 18										
Notes:								Final Score		

Date:	50	60	70	80	90	100	50	60	70	Tot.
Holes 1 - 9										
Holes 10 - 18										
Notes:								Final Score		

Date:	50	60	70	80	90	100	50	60	70	Tot.
Holes 1 - 9										
Holes 10 - 18										
Notes:								Final Score		

Date:	50	60	70	80	90	100	50	60	70	Tot.
Holes 1 - 9										
Holes 10 - 18										
Notes:								Final Score		

Pitching Accuracy Challenge

Date:	50	60	70	80	90	100	50	60	70	Tot.
Holes 1 - 9										
Holes 10 - 18										
Notes:									Final Score	

Date:	50	60	70	80	90	100	50	60	70	Tot.
Holes 1 - 9										
Holes 10 - 18										
Notes:									Final Score	

Date:	50	60	70	80	90	100	50	60	70	Tot.
Holes 1 - 9										
Holes 10 - 18										
Notes:									Final Score	

Date:	50	60	70	80	90	100	50	60	70	Tot.
Holes 1 - 9										
Holes 10 - 18										
Notes:									Final Score	

Date:	50	60	70	80	90	100	50	60	70	Tot.
Holes 1 - 9										
Holes 10 - 18										
Notes:									Final Score	

Pitching Accuracy Challenge

Date:	50	60	70	80	90	100	50	60	70	Tot.
Holes 1 - 9										
Holes 10 - 18										
Notes:									Final Score	

Date:	50	60	70	80	90	100	50	60	70	Tot.
Holes 1 - 9										
Holes 10 - 18										
Notes:									Final Score	

Date:	50	60	70	80	90	100	50	60	70	Tot.
Holes 1 - 9										
Holes 10 - 18										
Notes:									Final Score	

Date:	50	60	70	80	90	100	50	60	70	Tot.
Holes 1 - 9										
Holes 10 - 18										
Notes:									Final Score	

Date:	50	60	70	80	90	100	50	60	70	Tot.
Holes 1 - 9										
Holes 10 - 18										
Notes:									Final Score	

Dr Nicky Lumb

Pitching Accuracy Challenge

Date:	50	60	70	80	90	100	50	60	70	Tot.
Holes 1 - 9										
Holes 10 - 18										
Notes:									Final Score	

Date:	50	60	70	80	90	100	50	60	70	Tot.
Holes 1 - 9										
Holes 10 - 18										
Notes:									Final Score	

Date:	50	60	70	80	90	100	50	60	70	Tot.
Holes 1 - 9										
Holes 10 - 18										
Notes:									Final Score	

Date:	50	60	70	80	90	100	50	60	70	Tot.
Holes 1 - 9										
Holes 10 - 18										
Notes:									Final Score	

Date:	50	60	70	80	90	100	50	60	70	Tot.
Holes 1 - 9										
Holes 10 - 18										
Notes:									Final Score	

PERSONAL BESTS

Enter your first personal best when you started this workbook and your final score. Hopefully you've made great progress!

Landing Spots

PB Date:		
Total Shots		

Landing Spots - How Far Can You Go?

PB Date:		
Level 1		
PB Date:		
Level 2		

Chip and Runs - How Far Can You Go?

PB Date:		
Level 1		
PB Date:		
Level 2		

Achieve 9 Chips in the Scoring Zone

PB Date:		
Total		

Up and Down the Ladder

PB Date:		
Up		
Down		
Total		

Short, Middle and Long

PB Date:		
Level 1		
PB Date:		
Level 2		

Sand Landing Spots

PB Date:		
Total Shots		

Achieve 9 Sand Shots in the Scoring Zone

PB Date:		
Total Shots		

How Many Shots to Achieve 9 Up and Downs

PB Date:		
Total Shots		

Par 18

PB Date:		
Level 1		
PB Date:		
Level 2		

One Ball Chipping Challenge

PB Date:		
Score		

Chipping Accuracy Challenge

PB Date:		
Score		

Dr Nicky Lumb

Wedge Matrix Distances

PB Date:		
L1 Wedge		
Total Shots		
PB Date:		
L2 Wedge		
Total Shots		

Stock vs Random Moving - 50-100 Yards

PB Date:		
Level 1		
PB Date:		
Level 2		
PB Date:		
Level 3		

Stock vs Random Moving - 100-125 Yards

PB Date:		
Score		

Stock vs Random Static - 50-100 Yards

PB Date:		
Level 1		
PB Date:		
Level 2		

Stock vs Random Static - 100-125 Yards

PB Date:	
Score	

One Ball Pitching Challenge

PB Date:	
Score	

Pitching Accuracy Challenge

PB Date:	
Score	

Notes

Notes

Dr Nicky Lumb

Notes

Notes

Dr Nicky Lumb

Notes

Notes

Notes

Notes

Dr Nicky Lumb

Notes

Notes

Dr Nicky Lumb

**Congratulations on completing
Better Practice Better Golf
Short Game Workbook!**

For more information visit

BetterPracticeBetterGolf.com

Made in the USA
Las Vegas, NV
21 February 2022

44328344R00098